Model, **Rig, Animate**

with 3ds max 7

Michele Bousquet

New
Riders

Model, Rig, Animate with 3ds max 7

Michele Bousquet

New Riders
1249 Eighth Street
Berkeley, CA 94710
510/524-2178
800/283-9444
510/524-2221 (fax)

Find us on the World Wide Web at: www.peachpit.com
To report errors, please send a note to errata@peachpit.com

New Riders is an imprint of Peachpit, a division of Pearson Education
Copyright © 2005 by Michele Bousquet

Editors: Kate McKinley, Becky Morgan
Production Editor: Simmy Cover
Technical Editors: Nate Calef, Michael McCarthy
Compositor: Maureen Forys, Happenstance Type-O-Rama
Indexer: Irv Hershman
Cover design: Mimi Heft
Interior design: Maureen Forys, Happenstance Type-O-Rama

ISBN 0-321-32178-2

9 8 7 6 5 4 3 2 1

Printed and bound in the United States of America

Acknowledgments

Thank you to Michael McCarthy and Nate Calef for technical editing.

A big thanks to master animator Paul Neale for taking the time to show me his approach to rigging, and thus providing the foundation for the techniques in this book. Thanks also to Michael Comet for additional rigging tips.

Thanks to Precision Wordage, Inc., for proofing and other assistance.

And the biggest thank-you of all to my ever-patient husband David. A writer never had it so good.

PREFACE

This book focuses on the basics of modeling, rigging, and animating low-poly characters with 3ds max, a complete modeling, animation, and rendering software package by Discreet for the Windows operating system.

In recent years, 3ds max has become the mainstay modeling program for numerous game development, broadcast, and film companies. Artists at these companies use many of the techniques described in this book to create their animated scenes.

The need for this book became apparent to me during day-to-day work with new animators attempting to learn how to model and rig their own characters. There are a few free resources on the Internet that can show you how to make a specific model, plus a couple of books that cover the topics from A to Z, but I couldn't find a simple, to-the-point resource that taught the basics for creating a model and rig while paving a foundation for more complex work.

Modeling and rigging are crafts that can take months or years to master, but they can also be used by the novice to start creating simple, rewarding scenes. Animating one's own visions is perhaps the most inspiring part of working in 3D, and I am of the opinion that you can start right here, right now. There's no need to learn every tool in 3ds max before you get results.

This book focuses on the fundamental techniques, going step-by-step with each tool so you know how it should be used. By the time you're done with this book, you'll be able to model, rig, and animate simple characters of your own design, and you'll be in great shape to take advantage of more complex techniques presented in other resources, such as the texts listed at the end of this book.

With this book, you're just a few steps away from making your visions a reality. May the learning process be enjoyable for you, and may you become the animator you've always dreamed of being.

—Michele Bousquet

Contents

How to Use This Book

This book provides an introduction to low-polygon character modeling, rigging, and animation with 3ds max.

The book is divided into three sections:

- **SECTION 1: CHARACTER MODELING** Model a low-polygon character.

- **SECTION 2: CHARACTER RIGGING** Create bones and a fully functional rig for the character. Apply the Skin modifier and adjust its settings.

- **SECTION 3: ANIMATION** Use traditional principles of animation with 3ds max's tools to create finished animation for the character's face and body.

The book is designed so you can go through it from beginning to end to create a complete project. Alternatively, you can skip to sections that interest you. Numerous files are included on the CD that allow you to jump in just about anywhere and do the project.

In each chapter, you'll find:

- An explanation of the tools needed for the next task

- Optional Practice exercises

- Tutorial exercises for the project

Practice exercises are named with single alphabetical letters (A, B, C, and so on) that continue throughout the book. Tutorials are named with a letter to indicate the chapter, followed by a number. For example, the tutorials in the character modeling chapters start with M1, then M2; in the skinning chapter they're S1, S2, and so on.

If you want to skip the explanations and practice exercises and get right to the instructions, look for the Tutorials. If you want to use the techniques for your own project, read the explanation, do the Practice exercises, and use the techniques on your own model.

About the CD

The CD that comes with this book contains files used in practice exercises and tutorials. When you need to load a file, you are given the filename as well as the folder.

On the CD you'll find a number of snapshot files. These are files saved along the way during tutorials. When you're instructed to save a file with a particular filename, you'll find a matching file on the CD. Feel free to load these files at any time to study them or check your work.

The CD contains the following folders:

- *Animation* holds folders used in the *Animation* section (Chapters 6 and 7). It includes a *Scenes* folder with 3ds max scenes, and an *AVI* folder with rendered animations.

- *Models* holds the files for the *Modeling* section (Chapters 1 and 2).

- *Practice* holds practice scenes that you'll load for practice exercises throughout the book.

- *Rigs* contains files for Chapters 3 and 4 in the *Rigging* section.

- *Skinning* contains files for Chapter 5 in the *Rigging* section.

It is not necessary to copy files from the CD to your hard disk, but you can do so if you want.

Character Modeling

The tutorials throughout this book will lead you through a single project: to model, rig, and animate a simple character similar to the one shown. In this section, you'll model the character, piece by piece.

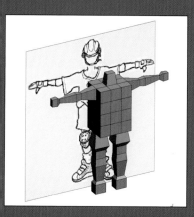

CHAPTER 1

Modeling the Body

The first step in the character animation process is the creation of a character body that will animate well.

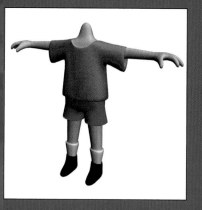

In this chapter, you'll model a character's body, similar to the one shown.

To prepare for modeling, create two folders on your hard disk to save your scenes as you go along. Create a *Practice* folder to hold the practice exercises you do in preparation for the real thing, and a *Models* folder to hold the models you create for the project.

Definitions and Terms

These terms are used in this chapter when describing the modeling process. You'll also find them frequently in the 3ds max documentation.

MODEL A three-dimensional (3D) representation created in a software package such as 3ds max.

FACE A flat, triangular area of a model. Models are made up of faces, and each face is surrounded by three lines called *edges*.

POLYGON A flat area of a model, usually rectangular, made up of two or more faces. A polygon is surrounded by edges, usually four but sometimes more. We'll be working mostly with polygons in this book.

VERTEX A point where two edges meet. The plural of vertex is *vertices*.

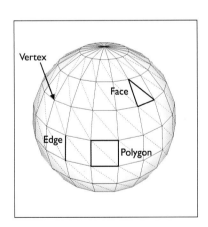

LOW-POLY A model is considered low-poly when it has relatively few polygons, which also means few faces and vertices. Low-poly models use less computing power, so they update more quickly in viewports and render faster than high-poly models. For this reason, low-poly models are used in real-time games. They are also used even when the final result will be high-resolution output, such as broadcast (TV) or film. In this case, the low-poly model is used during the animation phase, then a high-poly version is substituted just before rendering. Even with high-poly models, the fewer polygons you can use without sacrificing quality the easier the model is to work with.

BOX MODELING A modeling technique that starts with a primitive object such as a box or sphere. You can model just about anything with box modeling, including characters of any kind.

Reference Pictures

Before starting to model, you should have reference drawings or photos of the character you want to make. Taking the time to sketch out the character, even roughly, will save you hours of modeling time.

Some modelers find it useful to scan in one or two reference pictures and display them in 3ds max viewports when modeling. There are two ways you can go about this:

- Set up one or two planes and map the pictures onto them.

- Display each reference picture as a background in a viewport.

In this book we use the first method, using the picture shown here as a guide to the proportions for our character.

PRACTICE A

Displaying the Reference Picture on a Plane in the Scene

1. Choose *File > Reset* to reset 3ds max.

2. In the Front viewport, create a **Plane** object of any size. You can find the Plane creation command in the same place you find the Box and Sphere commands, on the default ![icon] **Create** panel.

    A plane is similar to a box, but it has no thickness. A plane is ideal for placing reference images in a scene.

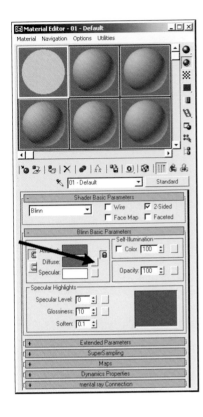

3. Press the **[M]** key to open the Material Editor.

4. In the Shader Basic Parameters rollout, check the **2-Sided** option.

   This will make the picture show up on both sides of the plane.

5. In the Blinn Basic Parameters rollout, under Self-Illumination, change the **Color** value to **100**.

   This will make the picture show up in the scene regardless of the amount or direction of the lighting.

6. In the Blinn Basic Parameters rollout, click the ☐ small box next to the Diffuse color swatch, and choose **Bitmap** from the Material/Map Browser. Select the file you want to use as a background. You can use any picture for practice.

7. Select the plane, and click 🖳 **Assign Material to Selection** on the Material Editor.

8. Turn on the 🌐 **Show Map in Viewport** option on the Material Editor.

   The picture appears on the plane in the Perspective viewport. You can make it appear in other viewports by right-clicking the viewport label and choosing *Smooth + Highlights* from the pop-up menu.

   If the reference image doesn't appear to have the correct proportions, you'll need to change the plane's length and width.

PRACTICE B

Displaying a Reference Picture as a Background

You won't use this method of displaying reference images in this book, but it's useful to know how to do it. You might find you prefer this method for your own scenes.

1. Choose *File > Reset* to reset 3ds max.

2. Activate the viewport in which you want the reference picture to appear.

3. Choose *Views > Viewport Background* to display the Viewport Background dialog.

4. Click **Files**, and choose the reference picture from the file selector dialog that appears. You can practice with any picture you like.

5. On the Viewport Background dialog, make sure the **Display Background** checkbox is checked.

6. Set **Aspect Ratio** to **Match Bitmap**, and check the **Lock Zoom/Pan** checkbox.

   When **Lock Zoom/Pan** is checked, the picture will zoom when you zoom the viewport. If you don't check this option, the picture won't zoom in or out along with your model, and it will be difficult to use the reference picture effectively.

7. Click **OK** to display the picture in the current viewport. Zoom in or out of the viewport to see the entire picture.

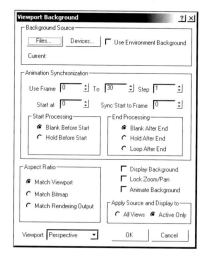

TUTORIAL M1

Displaying the Skater Reference Picture

Here, you'll display the reference picture *SkaterFront.jpg* on a plane in the Front viewport so you can use it as a guide when modeling.

Set up the Material

1. Locate the file *SkaterFront.jpg* in the *Models/Maps* folder on the CD. Copy this file to the *3dsmax7/Maps* folder on your hard disk.

2. In 3ds max, create a Plane in the Front viewport. Set its parameters as follows:

Length	410
Height	380
Length Segs	1
Width Segs	1

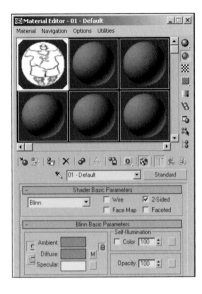

3. Press the **[M]** key to open the Material Editor.

4. In the Shader Basic Parameters rollout, check the **2-Sided** option.

5. In the Blinn Basic Parameters rollout, under Self-Illumination, change the **Color** value to 100.

6. In the Blinn Basic Parameters rollout, click the [ ] small box next to the Diffuse color swatch, and choose **Bitmap** from the Material/Map Browser. Select the file *SkaterFront.jpg*.

7. Click 🔲 **Assign Material to Selection** on the Material Editor.

Prepare Viewports for Modeling

1. Turn on the 🌐 **Show Map in Viewport** option on the Material Editor.

2. Right-click the Front viewport label and choose *Smooth + Highlights* from the pop-up menu.

    This makes the image visible in the Front viewport, where you will do most of your work.

3. Click 🔲 **Zoom Extents All**, located at the lower right of the screen.

    This shows the plane in all viewports.

4. Right-click the Perspective viewport label and choose *Texture Correction* from the pop-up menu.

    Turning on Texture Correction causes the system to use a small amount of extra resources to display the bitmap correctly.

5. To turn off the grid display in each viewport, activate each viewport and press the **[G]** key. This makes the reference picture easier to see.

6. Right-click the Front viewport label and choose *Edged Faces*. Do the same for the Perspective viewport.

    This will enable you to see the edges on the box after you create it.

Start with a Box

Most low-poly models start with a box primitive. As you gain experience with box modeling, you might find that a sphere or cone works better for some of your characters. In this book we focus on a human-type character, which is easier to create from a box than from a cylinder or sphere.

You'll smooth the box later, so very few polygons are needed at the start.

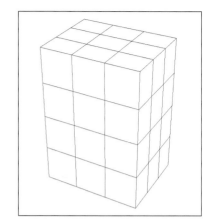

TUTORIAL M2

Creating the Initial Box

1. In the Top viewport, create a Box primitive. Set its parameters as follows:

Length	70
Width	90
Height	125
Length Segs	3
Width Segs	3
Height Segs	4

2. In the Top viewport, move the box downward so it sits in front of the plane.

3. In the Front viewport, move the box so the top of it aligns with the skater's shoulders in the reference picture.

Converting the Box

Before we begin the box modeling process, you'll convert the box to an Editable Poly or Editable Mesh. The conversion won't change the shape of the box, but it will change the way the box can be edited. You'll need these editing abilities to create the character.

When you create a box, you can go to the  Modify panel and change its Height, Length, and Width parameters. After you convert a box to an Editable Poly or Editable Mesh, you can no longer access these parameters. They'll be replaced by other tools that you can use to push and pull the box into shape.

An Editable Poly has slightly different tools than an Editable Mesh. For 95 percent of box modeling tasks, the tools are the same for both types of objects, but there are a few situations where the unique Editable Poly tools come in handy. You'll see the reason for using Editable Poly more clearly later on, when we get down to smoothing and modeling details.

TUTORIAL M3

Converting the Box to an Editable Poly

Now you'll convert your character's box to an Editable Poly.

1. With the box selected, go to the  **Modify** panel.

    This displays the modifier stack. The modifier stack currently has only one listing: Box.

2. Right-click the **Box** listing in the modifier stack, and choose *Editable Poly* from the pop-up menu.

    The box is converted to an Editable Poly, and the original box parameters are no longer accessible.

3. Change the name of the object to **Body**.

4. Save the scene in your *Models* folder with the filename **LPChar01.max**.

    The letters in the filename stand for "low-poly character."

▸TIP◂

It's a good practice to save your work often as you model the character. In the tutorials, you'll be instructed when to save, but you can save more often, if you like.

Shaping with Polygons

Once the primitive is converted to an Editable Poly, the first step is to form limbs off the main box. With box modeling, you form limbs by pulling new polygons out from the original box, a process called *extruding*.

Before you can manipulate polygons, however, you must access the Polygon sub-object level.

Accessing and Selecting Polygons

You can access the Polygon sub-object level in either of two ways:

- Click the [+] next to the Editable Poly listing on the modifier stack and choose *Polygon* from the list that appears.

- Click the 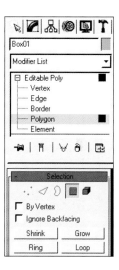 **Polygon** button on the Selection rollout.

Now you can select the polygons you wish to manipulate. Click any polygon, and you'll see the edges around it turn red to indicate that the polygon is selected.

You can select polygons in the same ways you select objects:

- Hold down **[Ctrl]** and click to select additional polygons.

- Hold down **[Alt]** and click to unselect polygons.

- Drag to create a selection region around polygons to select or deselect several at once.

To make the selected polygons appear as solid red, you can turn on the Shade Selected Faces Toggle. Press **[F2]** to turn this feature on and off.

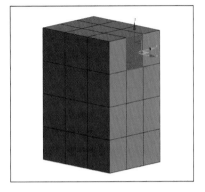

►TIP◄

Use Arc Rotate only in the User view-port. Using it in another viewport will turn that viewport into an angled User view. You don't need more than one User view onscreen at a time, and you need to retain your Top, Front, and Left views for accurate modeling. If you accidentally turn a Top, Front, or Left viewport into a User viewport, press [T], [F], or [L] on the keyboard to change the viewport back to its original display.

►TIP◄

If Arc Rotate causes the object to rotate out of view, try using Arc Rotate Selected instead. To do this, click and hold the Arc Rotate button until a flyout with three buttons appears. Choose the middle button, where the circle at the center of Arc Rotate is solid white. Now, when you rotate the view, the object will stay centered in the viewport.

PRACTICE C

Selecting Polygons

Here, you'll practice accessing the Polygon sub-object level and selecting polygons.

1. Before working on your scene, save the file as **PracticeC.max** in your *Practice* folder.

    This will prevent you from accidentally saving over your project file.

2. Hide the reference plane to make it easier to work with the box. To do this, select the plane with the reference picture, then right-click and choose *Hide Selection* from the Quad menu.

3. Change the Perspective view to a User view. To do this, activate the Perspective viewport and press the **[U]** key.

4. Press the **[F2]** key to turn on the Shade Selected Faces Toggle.

5. On the **Modify** panel, access the ■ **Polygon** sub-object level.

6. Select any polygons on the box.

    The polygons will turn a bright, solid red to indicate that they are selected. If they don't, press **[F2]** again to toggle the display.

7. In the User viewport, use [⟳] **Arc Rotate** to rotate the view. Hold down the **[Ctrl]** key and click polygons on another side of the box.

8. Continue selecting polygons until you can do it easily on any part of the box.

    Keep this file on your screen for use in the next practice exercise.

Extruding Polygons

Now that you can select polygons, you're ready to extrude existing polygons to create new ones, and form the limbs.

Locate the Extrude parameter on the Edit Polygons rollout. Click the 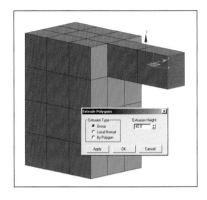 **Settings** box next to the Extrude parameter to display the Extrude Polygons dialog.

Change the **Extrusion Height**, and watch the viewport to see if you like the change. If so, click **Apply** to set the change.

After you click **Apply**, the extrusion height will be permanently added to the selected polygons, then a further extrusion with the same parameters will be displayed in viewports. This new extrusion won't be applied permanently until you click **Apply** or **OK**.

If you don't want to extrude the selected polygons any more, you can click **Cancel** to set the previously applied changes, or **OK** to set the currently displayed change in addition to previously applied changes. You can also select other polygons while this dialog is open and apply changes to them.

You can extrude and scale polygons at the same time by using the Bevel command. This command extrudes with the Height parameter, and scales the end of the extrusion with the Outline Amount. You can use a negative value as the Outline Amount to reduce the size of the extrusion end.

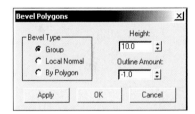

PRACTICE D

Using Extrude and Bevel

Here, you'll practice using these tools on your practice box, *PracticeC.max*. In the tutorial that follows, you'll reload the project file and create the arms for real on your character.

Extrude Polygons

1. Select the box you used in the last practice exercise. Go to the **Modify** panel, access the ■ **Polygon** sub-object level, and select some polygons.

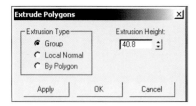

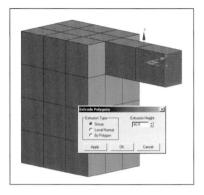

2. On the Edit Polygons rollout, click the **Settings** button next to Extrude. The Extrude Polygons dialog appears, and the **Extrusion Height** is temporarily applied to the selected polygons.

3. Change the **Extrusion Height** parameter, and press **[Enter]** so you can see the new temporary result.

4. Click **Apply**.

   The extrusion is permanently applied to the polygons, and a new extrusion is displayed on the selected polygons.

5. In any viewport, select a different set of polygons. As you select the polygons, note that the same **Extrusion Height** is temporarily applied to them.

6. Continue to experiment with the **Extrude** tool until you understand how it works. When you've finished, click **OK** to set the changes and close the dialog.

Bevel Polygons

1. Select a polygon that hasn't been extruded.

2. Click the 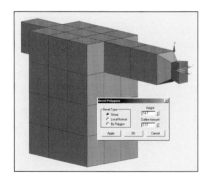 **Settings** button next to Bevel. The Bevel Polygons dialog appears.

3. Change the **Height** to 20 and the **Outline Amount** to –8 to cause the selected polygons to both extrude and scale.

4. Click **Apply**.

   At this point, the last extruded polygons might look somewhat pinched. The parameters you just applied to the originally selected polygons have been temporarily applied again, and this extreme scaling causes them to pinch.

5. Change **Outline Amount** to a positive number, causing the ends of the polygons to widen out. Click **Apply**.

6. Continue to experiment with the Bevel tool until you feel comfortable using it. When you've finished, click **OK** to exit the dialog and set the changes.

Creating the Arms

Now you're ready to apply what you've learned about polygons to your project. Here, you'll select two polygons on the box, one on each side, then you'll extrude them to form the character's arms.

Prepare the Scene

1. Load the file *LPChar01.max* that you created earlier. If asked if you want to save the current scene, click **No**.

    It's a good idea to freeze the reference plane so you don't select it by accident while modeling the character. Before you freeze it, you'll need to tell 3ds max not to turn it gray upon freezing.

►TIP◄

You can open a recently used file by choosing *File > Open Recent*.

2. Select the reference plane. Right-click the viewport and choose *Properties* from the Quad menu.

3. In the Display Properties group of the Object Properties dialog, turn off the **Show Frozen in Gray** checkbox. Click **OK** to close the dialog.

4. Right-click the viewport, and choose *Freeze Selection* from the Quad menu.

    The reference plane is still visible, but you can't select it. If you need to select it in the future, just right-click any viewport and choose *Unfreeze All*.

5. Change the Perspective view to a User view by activating the Perspective viewport and pressing the **[U]** key.

6. Press the **[F2]** key to display selected polygons in red.

Select Arm Polygons

1. On the **Modify** panel, access the **Polygon** sub-object level. Select the top center polygon on one side of the box.

    The polygon will turn a bright, solid red to indicate that it's selected.

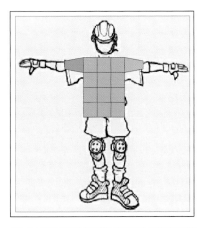

2. In the User viewport, use 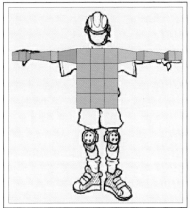 **Arc Rotate** to rotate the box around to the other side. Hold down the **[Ctrl]** key and click the corresponding polygon on the other side.

One polygon on each side of the box is now selected. Next, you'll extrude these polygons to make the arms.

Extrude the Arms

We'll use the **Bevel** tool to extrude the arms, since this tool offers the fastest workflow. We won't try to shape the clothing just yet—first we'll work on roughly shaping the body, then later we'll shape the clothing and other details.

1. Click the ▣ **Settings** button next to Bevel. The Bevel Polygons dialog appears.

2. Set **Height** to 40 and **Outline Amount** to –7. Click **Apply**.

You've just created the upper arms. Don't be concerned that the extruded arms don't exactly match the reference picture. We're using the picture as a guide for size, not necessarily for an exact match.

3. Enter these values on the Bevel Polygons dialog, and click **Apply** after you enter each set, creating four more beveled segments.

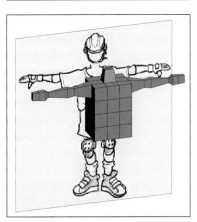

Body Part	Height	Outline Amount
Elbow	16	2
Lower Arm	45	–5
Base of Hand	9	5
Palm of Hand	15	–1

Here you'll extrude the neck. You'll create the head separately later, so for now you only need a neck extrusion for the head to sit on.

4. In the User viewport, select the neck polygon at top center of the box, where the head will protrude from the body.

5. If you closed the Bevel Polygons dialog, open it again. Set **Height** to 30 and **Outline Amount** to –4. Click **OK** to apply this extrusion and close the dialog.

6. Save the scene as **LPChar02.max**.

►TIP◄

To save a numbered file with the next incremental number, choose *File > Save As*, then click the plus sign **[+]** on the file selector dialog.

TUTORIAL M5

Extruding the Legs

Next, you'll extrude and shape the legs. You'll use the **Bevel** tool again, but this time you'll use it interactively rather than typing in specific values. You can use this tool interactively by clicking the **Bevel** button itself, dragging on selected polygons in a viewport to extrude them, then moving the cursor again to scale the end polygon.

1. In the User viewport, use [icon] **Arc Rotate Selected** to rotate the view so you can clearly see the bottom of the box.

2. Arrange the Front viewport so you can see where the character's legs will be.

3. Select the two polygons on the bottom that are directly below the arms. Refer to the picture to make sure you're selecting the right ones.

4. Click the **Bevel** button. Be sure to click the button that actually says **Bevel**, and not the **Settings** button you clicked earlier.

5. While watching the Front viewport, click and drag one of the selected polygons in the User viewport until the two extrusions reach the bottom of the character's shorts. Release the button, and move the mouse to flare the shorts slightly. Click to set the extrusion.

6. Click and drag again on the end polygons, and extrude to the tops of the knees. Release the button and scale the end polygons down to fit the knees. Click to set the extrusion.

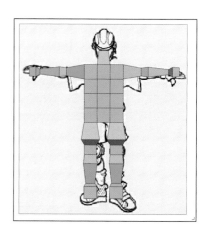

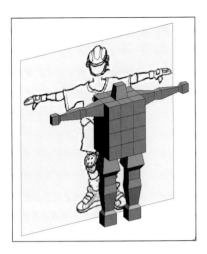

7. Continue extruding polygons to create the lower legs. When you reach the feet, simply extrude an ankle and a stump for now. You'll extrude the actual feet later on.

   Don't worry if your model doesn't look exactly like the one shown here. Box modeling takes practice! If you don't like the result, reload *LPChar02.max* and try again.

8. When you're satisfied with the model, turn off the **Bevel** button and save your work as **LPChar03.max**.

Shaping with Vertices

Extruding and outlining polygons will get you only so far in box modeling. At some point, you'll have to start moving vertices around to get the model into shape.

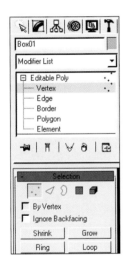

To work with vertices, you must first access the Vertex sub-object level. To do this, you can choose *Vertex* from the modifier stack, or click the ⸬ **Vertex** button on the Selection rollout. Then you can start selecting vertices and moving them around.

Characters are usually more rounded than boxy, so the first thing you'll want to do is smooth out the sharp corners. Then you can start shaping the body, arms, and legs to more closely match the reference picture.

To shape your model, work on one part at a time, such as the shoulders, chest, hips, or arms.

Select vertices as best you can in one viewport, then use other viewports to add or subtract from the selection. Move and scale vertices as necessary.

Always check more than one viewport to ensure you have the correct vertices selected before moving or scaling.

▶TIP◀

For the best results, use any viewport to select vertices, but use only the Top, Front, and Left viewports to move vertices, not the User or Perspective viewport. If you move vertices in the User and Perspective viewports, you can easily move vertices to unwanted places, then wonder why your model is crumpled or mangled.

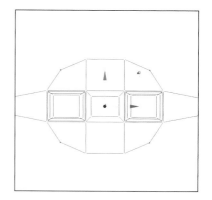

TUTORIAL M6

Shaping the Body's Vertices

1. Select the body, and access the 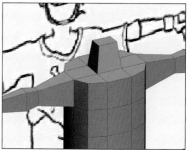 **Vertex** sub-object level.

2. In the Top viewport, use a selection region to select the vertices at the four outside corners of the box.

3. Scale the selected vertices inward on the XY plane to make the character body rounder.

4. Select the vertices at the base of the neck protrusion, and move them upward to create a shoulder area.

5. Select the vertices between the tops of the thighs (on the underside of the box), and move them downward to create a crotch area.

6. Select the vertices around each arm where the arm meets the shoulder, and scale these vertices away from the arm to smooth the transition from the body to the arms.

7. Work with the vertices on the model until it looks similar to the pictures shown.

8. Save the scene as **LPChar04.max**.

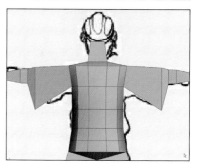

TurboSmooth

The beauty of low-poly modeling is that you can work with a very simple model, yet smooth it out quickly and effectively when necessary. Smoothing adds polygons to a model to smooth out sharp edges. Smoothing is best used for checking the model's shape or rendering the scene. When you're actively modeling or animating the character, you can turn the smoothing off to make your work much faster and easier.

Now that the box is starting to resemble a character, we can smooth it out and see how it's shaping up. There is a built-in smoothing option for Editable Polys, the Use NURMS Subdivision checkbox on the Subdivision Surface rollout. Although this option

works just fine, it's more convenient to perform smoothing with a modifier that you can turn on and off as you like.

A great new option for smoothing the model in 3ds max 7 is the TurboSmooth modifier. The advantage of using the TurboSmooth modifier is that you can turn it off quickly by clicking the light bulb next to the modifier on the modifier stack.

The new TurboSmooth modifier works similarly to the Mesh-Smooth modifier, which was available in previous versions of 3ds max and is still included with 3ds max 7. TurboSmooth has all the most-used options of MeshSmooth but it works a little faster, especially when it's the highest modifier on the stack.

TUTORIAL M7

Applying TurboSmooth to the Character

1. Apply the **TurboSmooth** modifier to the **Editable Poly** object.

2. In the Subdivision Amount rollout, set **Iterations** to 1 or 2.

    This smoothes out the model, but it doesn't appear to have any more polygons than it had before.

3. In the Local Control rollout, uncheck and check the **Isoline Display** checkbox, and note the change that occurs on the model.

    Turning off **Isoline Display** shows the edges for the actual polygons on the object. However, it's easier to work with this option turned on.

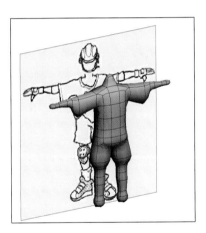

4. Turn on the **Isoline Display** checkbox.

    You can modify the object at the Vertex sub-object level while viewing the smoothed model.

5. Turn on the  **Show end result on/off toggle**.

    This will show the results of the **TurboSmooth** modifier no matter what level of the modifier stack is active.

6. Access the  Vertex sub-object level of the **Editable Poly** object. This makes it possible to move the object's vertices around while still seeing the smoothed result.

   Be sure to access the **Vertex** sub-object level for the **Editable Poly** object, not the **TurboSmooth** modifier.

7. Click the light bulb next to the **TurboSmooth** modifier to turn it off for now. You'll turn it on again later to help you check your work.

8. Save your work as **LPChar05.max**.

The Slice Tool

Currently, the areas where the clothing ends and the body begins are not well defined. This can't be solved simply by adjusting vertices, as there aren't enough vertices and edges to make the necessary detail.

This problem can be solved with the Slice tool. Slice divides a polygon, creating new edges and vertices for you to manipulate.

PRACTICE E

Using the Slice Tool

1. Reset 3ds max.

2. Create a cylinder in the Top viewport.

3. On the  **Modify** panel, right-click the cylinder listing in the modifier stack, and choose *Convert to Editable Poly*.

4. Set the Front and Perspective viewports to display *Smooth + Highlights* and *Edged Faces*.

5. Access the ⬛ **Polygon** sub-object level, and select the polygons at the center of the cylinder.

6. Click the **Slice Plane** button on the Edit Geometry rollout.

   A large yellow plane appears in the scene. This is the slice plane.

7. In the Front viewport, move and/or rotate the slice plane so it passes through the selected polygons in the place where you would like to cut the polygons.

   As you move the slice plane, you can see where the cut is going to take place by looking at the Perspective view. The location of the new edges changes as you move the slice plane.

8. When you're sure the slice plane cuts through the selected polygons, click the **Slice** button.

   New edges are cut where the slice plane passes through the selected polygons.

9. If you want to slice more polygons, move the slice plane and click **Slice** again.

10. When you're done slicing, be sure to turn the **Slice Plane** off.

    You can save this scene in your *Practice* folder if you like, but it isn't necessary.

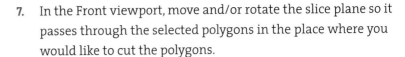

TUTORIAL M8

Slicing Detail on the Arms

Here you'll use the Slice tool to cut extra detail on the arm to help shape the clothing. You'll cut new polygons just below the elbow.

Prepare to Slice

1. Load the file *LPChar05.max* that you created earlier.

2. In the Top viewport, zoom in on the left arm.

3. Select the character's body.

4. Access the 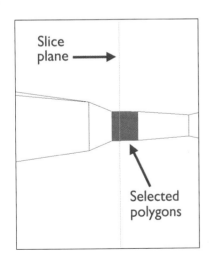 **Polygon** sub-object level.

5. Select the polygons in the elbow area.

Slice plane →

Selected polygons

Slice New Polygons

1. In the Edit Geometry rollout, click **Slice Plane**.

2. Move and rotate the slice plane so it passes through the selected arm polygons.

   When viewed in the Top viewport, the slice plane should appear as a single straight line.

3. Click **Slice**.

   New polygons have been cut for the upper arm.

4. Click **Slice Plane** to turn it off.

5. Select the same polygons on the opposite arm, and repeat the procedure to slice polygons on that arm.

6. Save your work with the filename **LPChar06.max**.

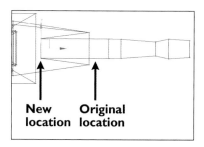

Shaping Overhangs

Now that you have more detail to work with, you can start to shape the overhanging parts of the clothing, such as the sleeves and pants legs. You do this by moving vertices near the clothing's openings inward past the sleeve or pants leg.

Ordinarily, you don't want to overlap vertices with their neighbors when box modeling. Shaping the overhangs is the exception. Perform this step carefully to avoid mangling your mesh.

►TIP◄

To ensure you select the polygons on the front, sides, and back of the arm, use a selection region when selecting the polygons.

TUTORIAL M9

Shaping the Sleeves

1. Access the 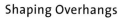 **Vertex** sub-object level of the **Editable Poly** object.

   Be sure to access the **Vertex** sub-object level for the **Editable Poly** object, and not for the **TurboSmooth** modifier.

2. Select the vertices at the elbow, the ones closest to the sleeve.

3. Move these vertices toward the torso and past the outer edge of the sleeve, as shown in the picture.

New location   Original location

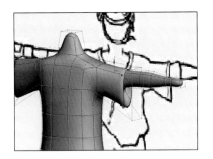

Take care to move the vertices well past their neighbors, and not right on top of other vertices. If you move vertices on top of one another, they'll be very hard to select later on.

4. Click the light bulb next to **TurboSmooth** to turn it back on.

5. On the modifier stack, click ⚎ **Show end result on/off toggle** to turn it on, if it's not already on.

6. Check the look of the smoothed model. You might have to move the selected vertices farther inward to fully shape the sleeve.

7. Repeat this procedure on the other arm to make another sleeve.

8. Check the sleeves in the Front viewport. If necessary, move the vertices around the edge of the sleeves to match them to the reference picture more closely.

9. Save your work with the filename **LPChar07.max**.

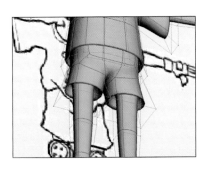

TUTORIAL M10

Shaping the Pants Legs and Shirt

You'll use the same method you used on the sleeves to form the pants legs and shirt hem. You can perform this procedure with TurboSmooth turned on or off.

1. If necessary, use the **Slice Plane** and **Slice** command to cut new edges just above or below the knee. You can select both legs at once, and slice the new edges on both legs at the same time.

2. Move the original knee vertices up inside the pants leg to form the cloth overhang.

   Be sure to turn on **TurboSmooth** to check that the vertices have been moved far enough to form the overhang.

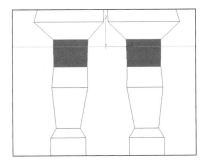

3. Check the model against the reference picture in the Front viewport. Move vertices as necessary to match the shorts in the reference picture.

4. Slice another set of edges around the area where the shirt meets the shorts.

5. Scale the new vertices to make a baggy shirt bottom, and move vertices to make the shirt overhang.

6. Save your work with the filename **LPChar08.max**.

The Hand

The next step is to add fingers to the hand. Rather than the four fingers on a regular human hand, we'll create a cartoon-style three-fingered hand with a thumb. This tradition started with Mickey Mouse and has continued into modern times with the characters in *The Simpsons* and the monsters in *Monsters, Inc.* The same techniques you use to make a three-fingered hand can be used to create four fingers, if that's the type of hand you prefer.

In shaping the hand, we'll work with just the left hand, then later on we'll mirror the hand over to the right side.

TUTORIAL M11

Creating the Thumb

You will first use **Bevel** to extrude the thumb from the hand.

1. Access the **Polygon** sub-object level.

2. Select the thumb polygon on the left hand.

3. Click the **Settings** button next to **Bevel**.

4. On the Bevel Polygons dialog, set **Height** to 7, and **Outline Amount** to –2. Click **Apply**.

5. Set **Outline Amount** to –1.5.

6. Click **OK** to set the change and close the dialog.

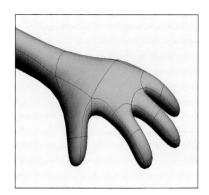

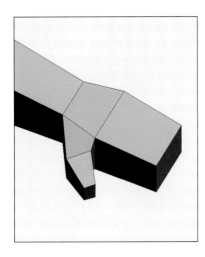

7. Access the  **Vertex** sub-object level. In the Top viewport, shape the thumb vertices individually to resemble the picture.

8. Save your work with the filename **LPChar09.max**.

Slicing Polygons for the Fingers

Here's yet another task where the Slice tool comes in handy. The Slice tool is excellent for creating the extra polygons needed for fingers, toes, and other protrusions.

The palm is not wide enough to accommodate three fingers, but you can easily fix that by scaling the polygon. However, there is another problem: You currently have only one polygon to extrude for the fingers. You need three fingers, so you'll have to use the Slice tool again to make more polygons for finger extrusions.

1. Using either the  **Vertex** or ▣ **Polygon** sub-object level, shape the left hand by moving or scaling until it looks similar to the picture.

2. Access the ▣ **Polygon** sub-object level. In the User viewport, select the polygon at the end of the hand.

3. Right-click the Left viewport label, and choose *Views > Right* from the menu.

   The selected polygon at the end of the hand now shows clearly in the viewport.

4. Click **Slice Plane**.

5. Rotate and move the slice plane so it cuts through the end of the hand about one third of the way over.

6. Click **Slice**.

7. Move the slice plane so it's about two thirds of the way over from the end of the hand. Click **Slice**.

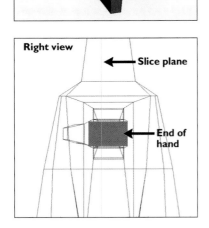

Right view

← **Slice plane**

← **End of hand**

8.   Click **Slice Plane** to turn it off.

     You now have three polygons at the end of the hand.

9.   Save your work as **LPChar10.max**.

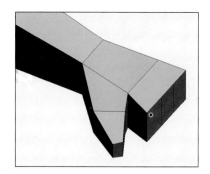

Extruding Multiple Polygons

We have our multiple finger polygons, and we're just about ready to extrude. Before doing this, we'll move the center finger vertices outward a little. This will cause the fingers to extrude outward from one another at an angle, making the fingers easier to select individually after they're extruded.

Now we're ready to extrude. You figure all you have to do is access the Polygon sub-object level, select the end finger polygons, extrude them, and…. Oh, no! The fingers extrude as one mass rather than as three individual fingers. Not a pretty sight.

Never fear, the Editable Poly is here. Remember when I said it had some advantages over an Editable Mesh object? One feature is that it can extrude multiple polygons separately rather than as one mass. We'll use this feature to extrude the fingers.

TUTORIAL M13
Extruding the Fingers

1.   Use the [icon] **Vertex** sub-object level to move the center hand vertices outward a little and prepare for finger extrusion.

2.   Access the [icon] **Polygon** sub-object level. Select the three finger polygons on the left hand.

3.   Open the Bevel Polygons dialog by clicking the **Bevel Settings** button. Select **By Polygon** as the **Bevel Type**.

     Turning on **By Polygon** will cause the polygons to extrude separately.

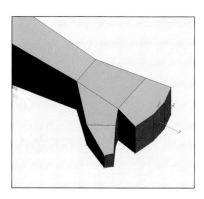

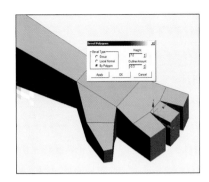

4. Change the **Height** value to 7 to make the first extrusion, and set **Outline Amount** to -0.3. Click **Apply**.

5. Set **Outline Amount** to -1.2. Click **OK** to apply this setting and close the dialog. (The cartoon-style fingers have only two segments.)

6. Turn on the **TurboSmooth** modifier to see how the fingers look.

7. Go to the **Vertex** sub-object level, and adjust the finger vertices as necessary to curl the fingers slightly and make a nice-looking hand.

8. Save your work with the filename **LPChar11.max**.

Detaching and Attaching Mesh Parts

Earlier, I mentioned that you should work on only one hand for the time being, as we would copy and paste the finished hand to the other side. To do this, you'll use the Detach tool to detach a copy of the geometry as a separate object, then use Attach to attach the copy to the other side.

TUTORIAL M14

Copying and Pasting the Hand

Detach and Copy the Left Hand

1. Turn off the **TurboSmooth** modifier if it's still turned on.

2. Access the **Polygon** sub-object level, and select all the polygons that make up the left hand.

3. On the Edit Geometry rollout, click **Detach**. The Detach dialog appears.

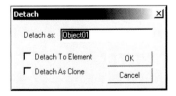

4. On the Detach dialog, check **Detach as Clone**. Enter the name **Right Hand** as the object name, and click **OK**.

   The left hand remains attached to the character and a new object, named **Right Hand**, appears in the scene.

Mirror the Detached Hand

1. Return to the **Editable Poly** level of the object. Otherwise, you won't be able to select the new Right Hand object.

2. Select the **Right Hand** object.

3. Make sure the Front viewport is active.

4. On the main toolbar, click 🔲 **Mirror Selected Objects**. On the Mirror Screen Coordinates dialog, make sure the **X** axis is selected, and click **OK**.

   The hand is mirrored across the center of the body, so the hand will always land in the correct place exactly on the other side of the body. If the hand doesn't align with the wrist, this means the wrist on the original body object should be adjusted, not the hand. You'll deal with this in later steps.

Delete the Original Hand Polygons

There are a few polygons on the right side of the body that make up the stub of the right hand. You'll now delete these polygons so you can attach the new hand to the wrist.

1. Select the body.

2. Access the 🔲 **Polygon** sub-object level.

3. Select the polygons that make up the stub of the right hand on the body.

4. Press **[Delete]** on the keyboard. When asked if you want to delete isolated vertices, click **Yes**.

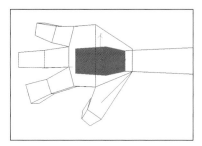

Weld the Wrist

Next, you'll attach the new right hand to the body and weld the wrist.

1. Access the 🔲 **Vertex** sub-object level.

2. Move the wrist vertices at the end of the arm to align with the hand's wrist vertices. Move them first in the Top viewport, then line them up in the Front viewport.

Now you'll attach the two objects together.

3. On the Edit Geometry rollout, with the body's wrist vertices still selected, click **Attach**, then click the new right hand.

   The hand is now part of the same object as the body. This will allow you to weld the vertices together at the wrist.

4. Click **Attach** to turn it off.

5. Select all the vertices at the wrist.

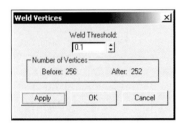

6. Click the ⬜ **Settings** button next to Weld. The Weld Vertices dialog appears.

   Under Number of Vertices, the **After** value should be exactly 4 less than the **Before** value, which indicates that by welding, you are going to reduce the 8 vertices in the wrist area (4 on the hand and 4 on the arm) to 4 vertices.

   If the **After** value isn't 4 less than the **Before** value, increase the **Weld Threshold** value until it is so. Alternatively, you can try moving vertices at the wrist closer to their corresponding hand vertices.

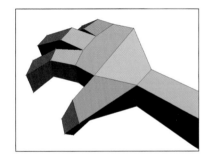

7. Click **Apply** to weld the vertices, then click **OK** to close the dialog.

   If all has gone well, the hands on both sides of the body now match.

8. Save your work with the filename **LPChar12.max**.

Modeling Details

Now that all the major body parts exist, we can start adding some
finishing touches. With what you know now, you can shape the
shoes, socks, and additional details. The fronts of the shoes can be
created with a simple extrusion from the front of the foot. The
socks and high-top sneakers can be shaped by slicing some new
edges and moving them up over neighboring edges, as you did
with the shirt and pants.

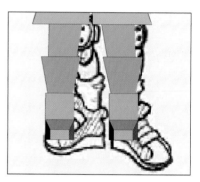

TUTORIAL M15

Shaping Socks, Shoes, and Body

Shape the Socks and Shoes

1. Extrude the polygons at the fronts of the feet to form the
    shoes.

2. Use the **Slice** tool to slice new edges near the knees.

3. Scale the new vertices so they're wider than the rest of the
    leg. Pull the wide vertices up past the adjacent vertices to
    form the socks.

4. Use the **Slice** tool to slice new edges near the ankles. Scale the
    new vertices to be wider than the rest of the ankle.

5. Move the vertices up to form the tops of the high-top
    sneakers.

Shape the Stomach and Shoulders

1. Shape the character's belly by moving the stomach and shirt
    vertices toward the center of his body in the Right viewport.

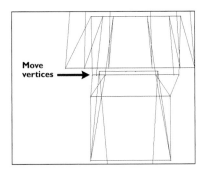

Move vertices →

2. The shoulders are also a bit boxy. Move the points between the armpits and chest downward and inward to round out the chest.

3. Check the model carefully to see if any other parts need adjustment. Use what you've learned to adjust the model for smoothness.

4. Save your work as **LPChar13.max**.

Creating New Edges

Our character is looking pretty good. Congratulations on getting this far! The only obvious thing lacking is a shirt collar. In order to make this shape, you're going to learn some advanced box modeling techniques.

To add the sleeve and pants detail, you sliced existing polygons and moved the vertices around. You could do the same to cut new edges for the shirt collar, but this would take a long time. Instead, you're going to create new edges in the shape of the shirt collar.

TUTORIAL M16

Shaping the Collar

Here, you'll cut new edges to create a collar shape.

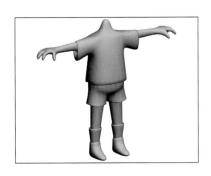

1. In the Right viewport, move the model farther away from the reference plane.

   This will enable you to reach the back of the model when cutting edges.

2. Remove the **TurboSmooth** modifier by highlighting it and clicking 🗑 **Remove modifier from the stack**.

3. Use 🔄 **Arc Rotate Selected** to rotate the User or Perspective view until you have a clear view of the model's shoulder area.

4. Access the ◁ **Edge** sub-object level. On the Edit Geometry rollout, click **Cut**.

5. In the User view, click the edges around the collar area to create new edges in a T-shirt collar pattern. Use the picture as a guide to where to click. Right-click to end the cut when you've finished cutting one set of edges.

6. Rotate the view with 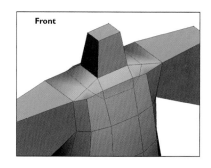 **Arc Rotate Selected** so you can work on the back of the model. Use **Cut** again to cut more edges in the pattern shown, and right-click to end the cutting action.

7. Click **Cut** to turn it off.

8. Check the collar edges in all viewports, and make adjustments as necessary using the 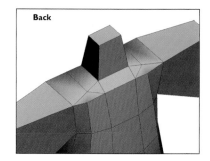 **Vertex** sub-object level.

9. Save your work as **LPChar14.max**.

Front

Back

Chamfer and Collapse

Now that you have edges to define the collar, you'll need an extra set of edges to pull inward and form the collar rim. This can be accomplished with the Chamfer tool. Chamfer makes two edges from one, splitting the two edges apart from the original location.

After performing a Chamfer, you might find that you need to clean up the model a little bit. Sometimes Chamfer leaves very small polygons, much smaller than the others around it, which can cause problems later on. You can fix these polygons by fusing two of the vertices around the polygon together with the Collapse tool.

TUTORIAL M17
Creating the Collar Rim

Chamfer the Collar Edge

1. Access the ⟨ **Edge** sub-object level.

2. Select the edges that form the collar, all around the front and back. The selection should form a continuous line all the way around the collar.

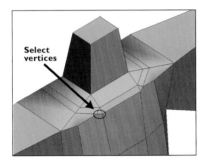

Select vertices

►TIP◄

If you have trouble selecting the correct vertices, you can try turning on the Ignore Backfacing option on the Selection rollout. This will prevent selection of vertices on the other side of the body.

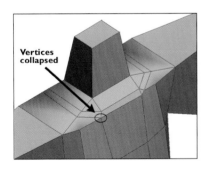

Vertices collapsed

3. Click the ▣ **Settings** button next to **Chamfer** on the Edit Edges rollout.

4. Increase the **Chamfer Amount** to about 2 to create the two edges, and click **OK**.

Clean up the Polygons

There is a little problem with the back of the collar. The chamfering process left two very small polygons at the back. Because these polygons are so small in comparison to the others around them, they will cause problems when you reapply **TurboSmooth**.

The **Collapse** tool fuses two vertices together, so you can use it to fix this problem. You can fuse two of the three vertices around the polygon together to change the triangle into a single edge.

1. Rotate the User view so you can see the back of the model.

2. Locate the two small faces formed by the collar rim.

3. Access the ▣ **Vertex** sub-object level.

4. Select the two vertices at the bottom of the triangular polygon.

5. On the Edit Geometry rollout, click **Collapse**.

   The two vertices are fused together, and the polygon is closed up.

6. Repeat this operation on the other polygon's vertices to close it up.

7. Save your work with the filename **LPChar15.max**.

Form the Collar Rim

Here you'll move the outer collar vertices to form the collar rim.

This is the tricky part. So far you've worked with edges and vertices that are relatively easy to see, select, and move. You'll need to learn a new technique for selecting and moving vertices to do this next step.

To properly form the collar rim, you'll need to rotate the User view with 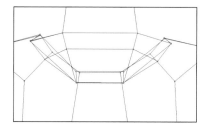 **Arc Rotate** to find and select vertices, then move the vertices in the Front or Left viewports. This process is sometimes tedious, and there may be times when you wonder if you'll ever understand what you're looking at. But it's important that you learn this technique and get the hang of it in order to move on to more advanced tools.

1. Access the ⣿ **Vertex** sub-object level.

2. Use ⣿ **Arc Rotate** to find the vertices that form the outer edge of the collar. Select each of the vertices.

3. Move the vertices upward, and scale them inward to fold over the collar.

You'll need to adjust the vertices manually to make the fold sit right. Eventually, you want the collar rim to look uniform, as shown in the picture.

4. In the Front viewport, locate an area that doesn't look right. Rotate the User view until you figure out where the errant vertices are, and select them right away in the User or Perspective view while you still know where they are. Then move the vertices in the Front or Left viewport.

5. Check your work by reapplying the **TurboSmooth** modifier with **Iterations** of 1 or 2 and looking at the collar rim. It should be smooth and uniform all the way around.

6. Save your work with the filename **LPChar16.max**.

This completes the modeling for the body. If you plan to animate the character, you might want to slice more edges at the knees and elbows to give the character more of an ability to bend his legs and arms. I'll leave that decision to you.

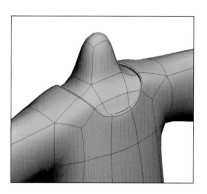

The Symmetry Modifier

In this book, you were instructed to build both sides of the character from scratch. However, you could have created one half and mirrored it to the other side with the Symmetry modifier.

Modeling with the Symmetry modifier has two advantages:

- You only have to model one half of the figure.

- The model is guaranteed to be symmetrical, which saves time during the rigging process.

This book instructed you to create both sides manually because you learned more tools that way—tools you'll need for more complex character modeling. In addition, when you're new to character modeling, it can be hard to visualize the entire character when you're working with only half of it.

If you want to try out the Symmetry modifier you can do so, but it's not necessary for finishing this particular character.

PRACTICE F

Using the Symmetry Modifier

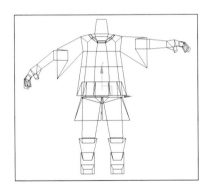

1. Load the latest version of the character model, and remove the **TurboSmooth** modifier from the body model.

2. Access the [ ] **Vertex** sub-object level. Alter some part of the model so you can see the effect of the **Symmetry** modifier in later steps. For example, you might move one of the arms up or down, or delete the left or right half of the model.

3. Exit the [ ] **Vertex** sub-object level.

4. Apply the **Symmetry** modifier to the body.

5. Access the **Mirror** sub-object level of the **Symmetry** modifier. To do this, click the [+] next to the Symmetry modifier and highlight the **Mirror** listing that appears.

6. Move the **Mirror** sub-object around to see the effect on the character. You'll need to turn on **Slice Along Seam**. You can also try different **Mirror Axis** settings, including **Flip**.

7. When the character looks the way you want it to, right-click the **Symmetry** modifier and choose *Collapse All* from the pop-up menu to turn the character into an **Editable Poly** again.

8. Reapply the **TurboSmooth** modifier.

9. If you like this version of the character better, feel free to save and use it for the next tutorial.

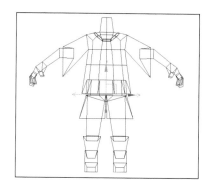

The Multi/Sub-Object Material

A Multi/Sub-Object material applies two or more materials to one object. This type of material is actually made of up several different sub-materials, each of which will be applied to different parts of the body.

TUTORIAL M18

Making a Material for the Body

Create the Material

1. Press [**M**] to open the Material Editor.

2. Select an unused sample slot.

3. Click the button labeled **Standard**, and choose **Multi/Sub-Object** from the Material/Map Browser.

   When asked if you want to discard or keep the current material, choose to discard.

4. On the Material Editor, click **Set Number**, and set the number to 5.

   Five materials are now displayed.

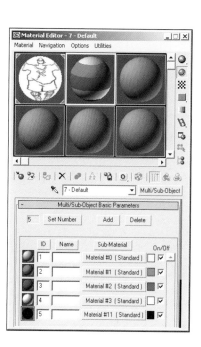

5. Click the color swatch at the far right of each material, and set colors as follows:

Material 1	Flesh tone
Material 2	Red
Material 3	Blue
Material 4	White
Material 5	Black

As you set the material colors, you'll see different-colored stripes appear on the sphere in the sample slot.

Set Material IDs

Now you need to tell 3ds max which parts of the body to apply each material to. This is accomplished with *material IDs*. By default, every polygon is assigned a material ID at the time the object is created. When you assign a Multi/Sub-Object material to an object, the material numbers correspond to the material IDs for the polygon.

Here, you'll set material IDs manually so different parts of the character receive different materials.

1. Select the body and access the ▢ **Polygon** sub-object level. Select all the polygons in the body.

   If you like, you can work with the ⴹ **Show end result on/off toggle** turned on so you can see how the selection affects the smoothed mesh. If you do so, keep in mind that you'll be selecting polygons displayed by the yellow cage, not the polygons on the mesh surface that were created by **TurboSmooth**.

2. In the Polygon Properties rollout, locate the **Set ID** value. Set this value to 1.

   This resets all the material IDs to 1, giving you a clean slate to work with.

3. Select the polygons that form the character's shirt, and change **Set ID** to 2.

4. Set material IDs for the remaining character parts as follows:

Pants	3
Socks	4
Shoes	5

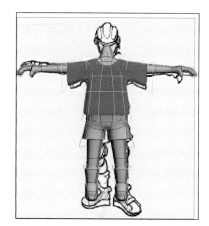

5. In the modifier stack, go to the **Editable Poly** level for the body.

6. On the Material Editor, click **Assign Material to Selection**.

    This applies the Multi/Sub-Object material to the body. The colors of the polygons on the body now correspond to the colors in the Multi/Sub-Object material, matched up by material ID.

    Check around the collar and pants legs to ensure you've set all the material IDs correctly.

    The body model is now complete!

7. Save your work with the filename **LPChar17.max**.

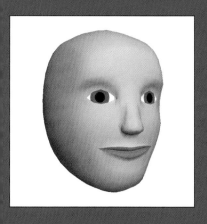

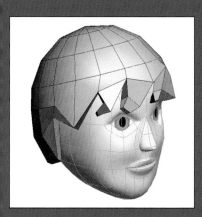

CHAPTER 2

Modeling the Head

Creating a low-poly head is a task that demands patience and practice. If you've ever tried to draw a realistic face or sculpt one in clay, you know that reproducing the human face is not a trivial task. Add to that the limitations of a low polygon count, and you can imagine the challenges that lie ahead.

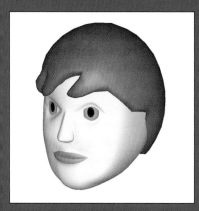

In this section, I'll walk you through the steps for making a low-poly head that resembles an action figure or doll. Making a photo-realistic head takes many more steps, but uses the same tools.

We'll create the face in a separate scene, then merge it into the body scene later on. When doing the tutorials in this section, don't be discouraged if your results don't come out quite as expected. Simply load the last file and try again.

Practice is the watchword here. Just as you wouldn't expect your first clay-sculpting attempt to look perfect, so it is with low-poly face modeling.

Reference Materials

As with the character's body, you would do well to use reference materials when modeling a low-poly face. Action figures, toys, and dolls are particularly good references for low-poly faces as they do a great job of representing the human face without a lot of detail.

Personally, I have a collection of figures from favorite animated films such as *Toy Story* and *The Little Mermaid,* plus a few Warner Brothers characters. If you visit your local fast-food chain when they're running a film or cartoon promotion, you can gather up quite a number of figures for the meager cost of a burger and fries.

There are a few rules to keep in mind when modeling heads:

- Place the eyes about halfway down the head.

- Exaggerated features make a character look more cartoony. For example, most cartoon characters have large eyes.

- Detailed facial features such as nostrils and earlobes can be simplified or left out on a low-poly character.

Here's a rendering of the low-poly head we'll create in this book. I used a combination of action figures to determine what the face would look like.

The Spherify Modifier

You might think that facial modeling would start with a sphere. However, I've found that the arrangement of faces on a sphere is not the best for face models. A box works much better. We'll apply the Spherify modifier to the box to form it into a spherical shape, then smooth the box's edges and mold the object into a head shape.

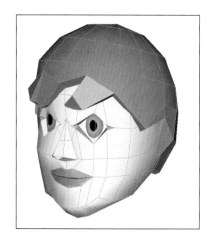

TUTORIAL M19

Creating the Head

1. Reset 3ds max, saving any changes to the body that you have recently made.

2. In the Top viewport, create a box of any size.

3. Go to the  **Modify** panel.

4. Change the parameters to the following:

Length	70
Width	70
Height	70
Length Segs	4
Width Segs	6
Height Segs	5

Figuring out how many segments to put on a box for a low-poly model requires a bit of guesswork. I settled on this arrangement by trial and error.

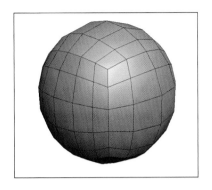

5. Apply the **Spherify** modifier to the box.

   The box is now shaped like a sphere.

6. Right-click the **Spherify** listing on the modifier stack and choose *Collapse All* from the pop-up menu. If a message appears asking to you confirm that you want to collapse, click **Yes**.

   The model is collapsed to an Editable Mesh.

7. Right-click the **Editable Mesh** listing and choose *Convert to Editable Poly*.

   Now you have a sphere-shaped box converted to an **Editable Poly**, and ready to be shaped into a head.

8. Save the scene as **LPHead01.max**.

Smoothing Groups

You may have noticed something about this spherified box—in a shaded view, you can clearly see the edges of the original box. This is due to something called *smoothing groups*.

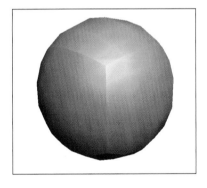

When an object is created, each face is assigned one or more smoothing group numbers. When the object is shaded or rendered, 3ds max compares each face's smoothing group number against the adjacent faces' numbers.

If the numbers on two adjacent faces match, 3ds max makes a smooth transition between the colors of the two faces, making the area look round and smooth. If the numbers don't match, 3ds max makes no effort to smooth the color transition, and the edge between the two faces appears hard.

Smoothing group numbers are assigned automatically when an object is created. When a box is created, all the faces on one side of the box are assigned to smoothing group 1, the faces on the next side are assigned to smoothing group 2, and so on. This causes each side of the box to look smooth while the edges between sides look hard and sharp. This is not desirable for a sphere, especially one that's used to model a face. You want the surface to look smooth all the way across.

Smoothing groups can be changed at the Face or Polygon sub-object level of an Editable Mesh or Editable Poly. Changing smoothing groups affects only the way the model is shaded and rendered, not the model's shape.

Note that a face can belong to more than one smoothing group. In other words, each face can have more than one number associated with it.

TUTORIAL M20

Smoothing and Shaping the Head

Smooth the Head Object

1. Access the ■ **Polygon** sub-object level.

2. Select all polygons on the object by drawing a selection region around it.

3. On the Polygon Properties rollout, in the Smoothing Groups section, click the button labeled **1**.

    All selected polygons are assigned to smoothing group 1, and the sphere looks smooth.

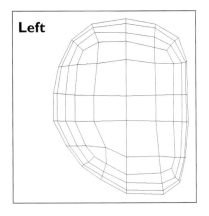

Left

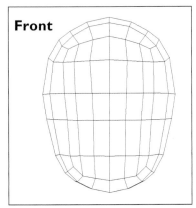

Front

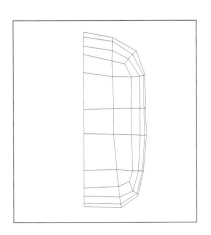

Shape the Head

The first step in making a character's head is to form the sphere into the rough shape of the head. This should be done before starting to model any of the character's facial features.

Imagine what your character's head would look like without eyes, nose, or mouth. This is the type of shape we want to achieve with the sphere before continuing. The easiest way to do this is to shape the head at the Vertex sub-object level.

There are no special tricks for this task, just a little work and some patience.

1. Access the [icon] **Vertex** sub-object level.

2. Move, rotate, and scale vertices until the head looks like an action figure head without eyes, nose, or mouth. Use the pictures as a guide.

3. Save your work as **LPHead02.max**.

Prepare to Make the Facial Features

Most of your work will focus on the front part of the sphere, where you'll mold and shape the eyes, nose, and mouth. You won't need to work on the back of the head for some time.

Since you'll be selecting a lot of vertices, edges, and polygons, and you don't want to accidentally select the back of the head when you want the front, you can make your work easier by hiding the polygons at the back of the head.

1. Access the [icon] **Polygon** sub-object level.

2. In the Top or Left viewport, select all the polygons that make up the back half of the head.

3. On the Edit Geometry rollout, click **Hide Selected**.

The polygons at the back of the head are hidden, along with their vertices and edges. This will make them impossible to select by accident.

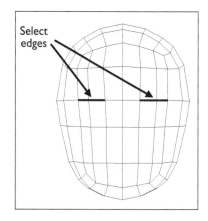

4. Save your work as **LPHead03.max**.

Creating Facial Details

OK, now comes the fun part. You'll start making the face by defining areas for the eyes, nose, and mouth.

In modeling the body, you learned that the Chamfer tool can be used to create two edges from one. You'll use this tool to make more edges for the facial features.

Since you know how to use Chamfer, I won't give you all the instructions in detail. You can either click **Chamfer** and do it that way, or use the **Settings** button next to Chamfer.

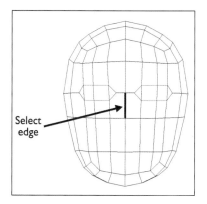

TUTORIAL M21

Defining the Facial Features

1. Access the [icon] **Edge** sub-object level.

2. Select the edges for the eyes, as shown in the picture.

3. **Chamfer** with an amount of about 4 to make the shapes for the eyes.

4. Select the edge for the nose, as shown in the picture.

5. **Chamfer** to about 3.

6. Select four edges for the mouth, as shown in the picture.

7. **Chamfer** to about 3.

8. **Chamfer** again to a little less than 3, just large enough to form lips, but so the new lip chamfer lines don't overlap each other.

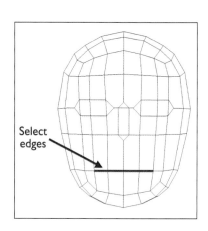

9. Save your work as **LPHead04.max**.

Eye Sockets

The best place to begin shaping detail is the most recognizable feature of a humanoid face—the eyes. Eyes are more than just holes in the head. They have an almond shape and are almost pinched at the corners.

TUTORIAL M22

Shaping the Eye Sockets

First you'll adjust the vertices that form the eye shapes, then you'll do a little extruding to form the eye socket and eyeball areas.

Make the Basic Eye Shape

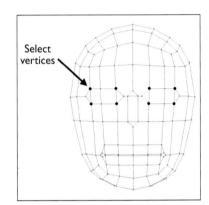

Select vertices

1. Access the Vertex sub-object level.

2. Select the second and fourth column of vertices on each eye, as shown.

3. In the Front viewport, scale the vertices vertically by about 50%.

4. Access the Polygon sub-object level.

5. Select all the polygons that make up the eyes.

6. Use **Bevel** to change the **Height** to -3, then set **Outline Amount** to -1.5.

7. Select the vertices at the centers of the eyes. In the Front viewport, scale these vertices vertically to about 200%.

8. Apply the **TurboSmooth** modifier to the head, with **Iterations** set to 1.

   The eye sockets are pinched at the corners, but they're starting to take shape.

9. Save your work as **LPHead05.max**.

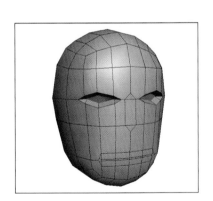

Fix the Pinches

The pinching problem that has developed around the eyes is not unusual when box modeling, especially when you've created new edges with the Chamfer and Bevel tools. You can see the problem most markedly when you turn on TurboSmooth and turn off Isoline Display.

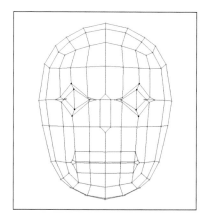

In general, pinching occurs when two or more vertices are too close to one another. The solution, fortunately, is simple. Chances are you only need one vertex at that spot, so you can simply collapse the vertices into one, and get fewer polygons in the bargain.

Finding the place where the vertices are close together is the trickiest part of this process. You'll have to find the vertices and select them before you lose track of them.

1. Turn off **TurboSmooth** if it's still turned on.

2. Access the ⬚ **Vertex** sub-object level of the Editable Poly.

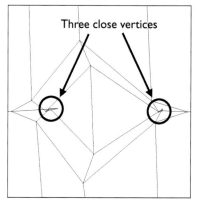

Three close vertices

3. In the Front viewport, zoom in on one of the eyes. Locate the places at each corner where three vertices are tightly grouped together.

4. Select one group of three vertices, and click **Collapse** on the Edit Geometry rollout.

5. Select the other group of three vertices, and click **Collapse** again.

6. If you want to see the effect this has had on the eye pinching, turn on **TurboSmooth** and view the eyes in the Front viewport. Do you see the difference between the two eyes? The collapsed side is much cleaner.

   Turn off **TurboSmooth** when you're ready to continue.

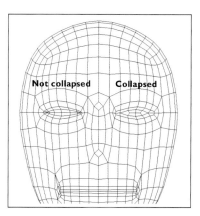

Not collapsed   Collapsed

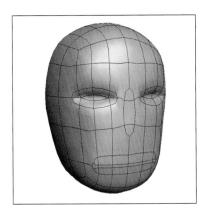

7. Repeat the collapsing process on the other eye.

8. Check your work carefully to ensure you haven't collapsed too many vertices.

9. Save your work as **LPHead06.max**.

Nose Detail

The nose needs more detail. You'll add the detail by cutting edges, then extruding the polygons to start making the nose. Once the nose is extruded, you'll collapse some of the vertices to remove unnecessary detail.

TUTORIAL M23

Shaping the Nose

You'll start by using the Cut tool to add more detail to the nose.

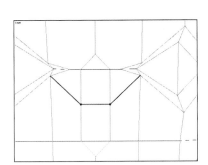

Cut New Detail

1. Access the **Edge** sub-object level.

2. Click **Cut**. Click at the center of each of the two longest nose edges to create two new edges.

3. Click at the lower inside corner of one eye, then click on the nose edges, then click on the opposite eye's corner to create the new detail, as shown in the picture.

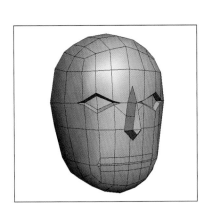

Bevel the Nose

1. Access the **Polygon** sub-object level.

2. Select the four nose polygons.

3. Use **Bevel** to increase **Height** to 2, and **Outline Amount** to 1.

4. Increase **Height** to about 4, and change **Outline Amount** to –2.

5. Save your work as **LPHead07.max**.

Remove Detail

You currently have much more detail than you need to make the nose. Let's collapse some vertices and make things less complicated.

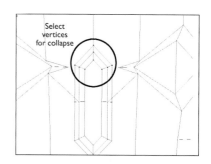

1. Access the 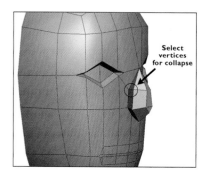 **Vertex** sub-object level.

2. Select all the vertices at the top of the nose. Click **Collapse**.

3. In the User view, zoom in to the middle part of the nose and rotate around until you can see the middle side vertices on one side of the nose. Select the two vertices as shown in the picture, and click **Collapse**. Repeat for the other side of the nose.

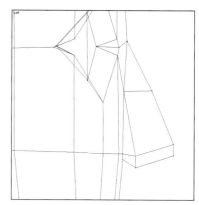

4. In the Left viewport, adjust vertices for a nice-looking profile.

5. Apply the **TurboSmooth** modifier and check your work. Make any further adjustments necessary to make the nose look good. For example, you can scale the vertices at the tip of the nose horizontally in the Front viewport to make a wider nose.

6. Save your work as **LPHead08.max**.

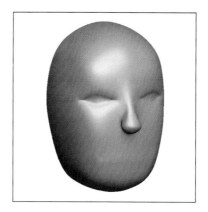

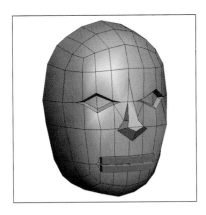

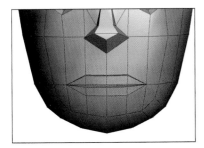

The Mouth

After all your work on the eyes and nose, shaping the mouth is relatively simple. It's just more of the same: extruding and collapsing.

TUTORIAL M24

Extruding the Lips

1. Turn off **TurboSmooth** if it's still turned on.

2. Access the 🔲 **Polygon** sub-object level. Select the eight polygons that make up the lips.

3. Use **Extrude** with **Extrusion Height** set to 2, and extrude the lips.

4. Access the ⬚ **Vertex** sub-object level. Select all the vertices at one corner of the mouth, including the vertices at the top and bottom of the lips. Click **Collapse**. Repeat for the other side of the mouth.

5. Turn on **TurboSmooth**, and make any necessary adjustments to the lips. For example, in the Front viewport, you can select all mouth vertices all the way across the head, and move them upward to move the mouth closer to the nose. You can also move the mouth vertices individually to shape the lips.

6. Save your work as **LPHead09.max**.

Finishing the Head

The basic face is complete. Now you only need to tidy up the head and make fine adjustments to the shape of the head and face.

Clean up Extra Vertices

At the back of the head, there is nearly as much detail as there is at the front. This level of detail is not really necessary to define the basic round shape of the head, especially since most of it will be covered with hair.

One easy way to reduce the number of polygons on the head is to collapse vertices at the back of the head using the Collapse tool under the Vertex sub-object level.

Edge Loops

You'll very likely want to animate the mouth and eyes at some later time. For smooth deformation of the mouth, you can use *edge loops*.

Edge loops are a series of edges that form a seamless loop. Edge loops around circular or oval body parts, such as the eyes and mouth, make deformation easier.

You can create edge loops by using the Cut tool under the Edge sub-object level to create new edges, and the Remove tool to remove edges you don't want.

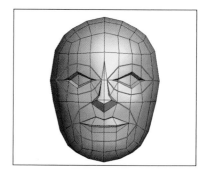

You can also test your loops by selecting an edge and clicking Loop on the Selection rollout. The Loop tool selects edges that touch end-to-end and pass through a junction of four edges. The Loop option provides a quick way to see how far your edge loops go.

TUTORIAL M25

Finishing the Head

Reduce Polygon Count

1. Turn off **TurboSmooth** if it's still turned on.

2. Access the ▣ **Polygon** sub-object level.

3. On the Edit Geometry rollout, click **Unhide All** to unhide all polygons.

4. Access the ⋮ **Vertex** sub-object level.

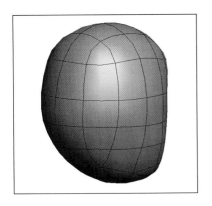

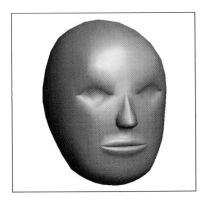

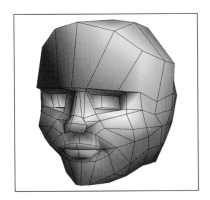

5. In the Selection rollout, turn on **Ignore Backfacing**.

   This will prevent you from selecting vertices on the side of the head opposite the one you're looking at.

6. Use **Arc Rotate** to look at the back of the head in the User viewport.

7. On the back of the head, select a pair of vertices to collapse. Check at the bottom of the Selection rollout to make sure only two vertices are selected.

8. Click **Collapse**.

9. Continue to choose pairs of vertices, and collapse each pair once it has been selected. Take care when selecting vertices to ensure you don't select the wrong ones before collapsing.

   This process takes a while, but you will be rewarded with a much lower polygon count for the head.

Improve Facial Details

1. Make any other adjustments that you wish to the face and head. For example, you can move the eyes closer together, or shape the cheekbones and chin. If you like, you can also create edge loops around the eyes and mouth.

2. If you make extensive changes to the face, use the **Symmetry** modifier to copy the changes from one side of the face to the other. When you've finished making changes, highlight the **Symmetry** modifier on the stack, then right-click and choose *Collapse To* to collapse the **Symmetry** modifier into an Editable Poly.

3. When you're done changing the face, save your work as **LPHead10.max**.

Creating Facial Materials

In the same way you used a Multi/Sub-Object material for the body, you'll also create and apply several materials for the face. You'll use a Gradient Ramp map to make the pupils of the eye.

TUTORIAL M26

Creating Materials for the Face

Set Material IDs

1. Access the ▣ **Polygon** sub-object level.

2. Select all the polygons on the head. On the Polygon Properties rollout, change **Set ID** to 1.

3. Select the polygons that make up the whites and pupils of the eyes. There are two polygons for each eye. Set the ID to 2.

4. Select the polygons that make up the fronts of the lips. Set the ID to 3.

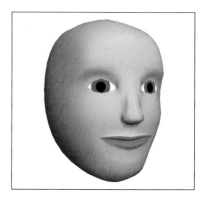

Set Colors for Skin and Mouth

1. Open the Material Editor. Select an unused material slot. Click **Standard** and pick **Multi/Sub-Object** from the Material/Map Browser. Click **Set Number** and set the number to 3.

2. For the first material, click the color swatch and change the color to a skin tone.

3. Copy this color to the color swatch for the third material. Change the color for the third material to a slightly darker or redder color, for the lips.

Create Eye Material

The material for the eyes will take a bit more work, as we need to create a special map to represent the eyeballs. You'll use a Gradient Ramp map to create a simple eye map from scratch.

1. Click the second material in the **Multi/Sub-Object** material.

2. For the Diffuse map, select the **Gradient Ramp** map.

3. Change the **Gradient Type** to **Radial**.

4. Set **Interpolation** to **Solid**.

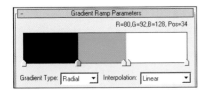

5. Set up the gradient to include blue, black, and white as shown in the picture.

   The gradient works with small markers called *flags*. You can add a new flag by clicking the gradient, or change a flag's color by double-clicking it. The gradient ramp is created between adjacent color flags.

6. Click  **Show Map in Viewport**.

   The map doesn't show in viewports just yet because there are no mapping coordinates assigned to the eyes.

Apply Mapping Coordinates

Mapping coordinates tell a map how to lie on the object. With a Gradient Ramp map, you have to tell the map how to align with the eyes. You do this with the UVW Map modifier.

1. Select the polygons that make up the whites and pupils for each eye, four polygons in all. In the Front viewport, scale these polygons vertically a little bit to make the eyes bigger.

2. Without exiting the **Polygon** sub-object level, select the **TurboSmooth** modifier on the stack. Apply the **UVW Map** modifier at this level.

   This will cause the default planar UVW Map gizmo to fit itself to the eyes automatically.

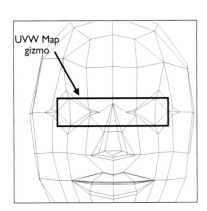

3. Activate the Front viewport and click **View Align** on the command panel.

   The **UVW Map** gizmo should now be positioned around the eyes, as shown in the picture. In addition, the eye map should now appear in shaded viewports.

4. Turn on **TurboSmooth** if it's not already on.

5. Working with the smoothed model, adjust the **U** and **V Tiling** and **Offset** values for the Gradient Ramp map until the eyes are the correct size, and appear to look straight ahead in the Front viewport. You can also adjust the sizes of the black and blue areas of the gradient if necessary.

6. Save your work as **LPHead11.max**.

►TIP◄

Try these values as a starting point for the Gradient Ramp:
U Offset: 0
V Offset: 0.1
U Tile: 3
V Tile: 0.5

Creating the Hair

You can create low-poly hair in a number of ways. This particular method uses a sphere, with extruded polygons representing tendrils or wisps of hair on the forehead.

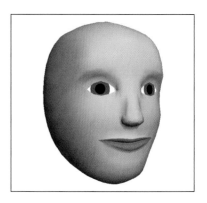

TUTORIAL M27

Creating the Hair

Create the Hair Object

1. In the Top viewport, create a sphere about the size of the character's head. Set **Segments** to 16 and **Hemisphere** to 0.53.

2. Move and rotate the sphere so it sits right on the character's head like a skull cap. Scale the sphere as necessary to make it closely fit the character's head.

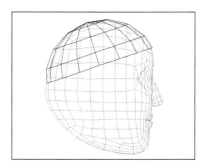

3. Convert the sphere to an Editable Poly.

4. Access the ▣ **Polygon** sub-object level.

5. Select all the polygons that make up the rounded portion of the sphere.

6. Click the Bevel ▣ **Settings** button. Choose **Local Normals** as the **Bevel Type**. Set **Height** to about 8 to make a helmet shape around the head, and click **OK** to exit the dialog.

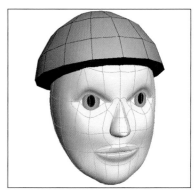

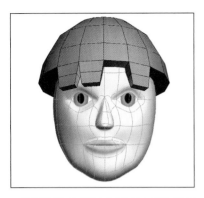

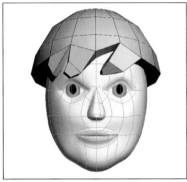

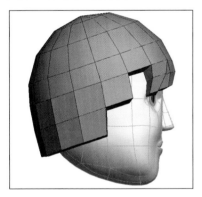

►TIP◄

You can make the hair as long as you like by extruding a few more times.

Create Tendrils

1. Select three or four polygons on the flat part of the hemisphere near the character's face.

2. Use **Bevel** to extrude the polygons. Be sure to set the **Bevel Type** to **By Polygon** to cause the tendrils to separate as they extrude. Extrude twice so you have some polygons for bending the tendrils.

3. Use the **Vertex** or **Polygon** sub-object level to shape the wisps to look like clumps of hair brushed away from the face. You'll need to check your work in all viewports to ensure the wisps fall close to the head.

4. Select polygons on the flat part of the hemisphere around the sides and back of the head. Extrude these polygons to form the rest of the hair, using the **Group** method for the **Bevel Type** or **Extrusion Type**.

5. Shape the hair as you like. To check your work, apply the **TurboSmooth** modifier with **Iterations** set to 1 or 2.

6. Apply an appropriate color or material to the hair.

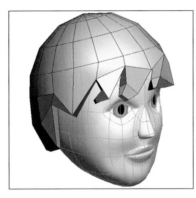

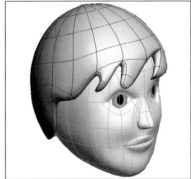

Merging

Now that you have a head and a body, you can merge the two. Merging will be a lot easier to deal with if we first name the objects appropriately.

TUTORIAL M28

Merging the Head and Body

Name Objects and Materials

1. Name the hair object **Hair**, and name the head object **Head**.

2. Press **[M]** to open the Material Editor, and select the head material. Click  **Go to Parent** until you reach the root level of the material. Change the name of the material to **Head Material**.

3. If you applied a material to the hair, change the material name to **Hair Material**.

4. Save your work as **LPHead12.max**.

5. Load *LPChar17.max*, the latest file containing the character body.

6. In the Material Editor, select the body material, and name it **Body Material**.

Merge Objects

1. Choose *File > Merge*, and select the file *LPHead12.max*.

2. In the Merge dialog, select both the **Hair** and **Head** objects to merge them into the current file.

    The head and hair come into the current scene.

3. Position the head and hair on the body. Scale the head and hair if necessary.

4. If the flesh tone colors on the head and body don't match, adjust the materials in the Material Editor.

5. Turn on **TurboSmooth** to see how the materials look on the smoothed body.

6. Save your work as **LPCharFinal.max**.

You Made It!

Congratulations! You have finished creating a low-poly character using both basic and advanced techniques in 3ds max. Feel free to learn more, experiment, and become a low-poly modeling expert.

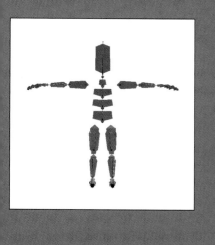

Character Rigging

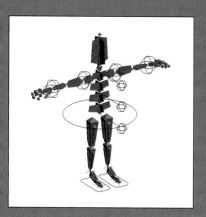

Now that your model is finished, you *could* animate it by animating its vertices, but animation goes much more quickly and easily if you first give your character a set of controls, known as a *rig*. A rig can be likened to the strings on a marionette, or wires inside a clay model—but 3D rigs are much more robust and complex than these physical counterparts.

Although it takes time to set up, a well-constructed rig makes the animation process much faster and easier.

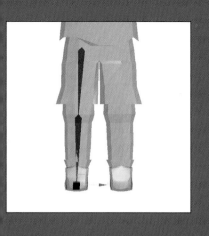

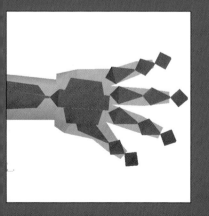

CHAPTER 3

Bones

Right now, your model is like a clay sculpture, with no easy way to make the parts move together realistically. So in this chapter, we'll give it a complete skeleton.

Terms and Concepts

Before we start, let's go over the rigging terms we'll be using in this chapter.

Linking

Linking creates a relationship between two objects, allowing you to control one object by moving or rotating the other.

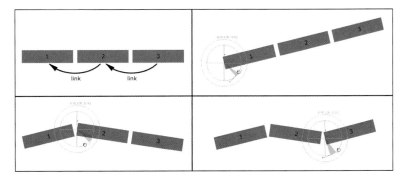

In the illustration, box 2 is linked to box 1, and box 3 is linked to box 2.

- Rotate box 1: All three boxes rotate.

- Rotate box 2: Boxes 2 and 3 rotate.

- Rotate box 3: Only box 3 rotates.

Linking is a standard feature in 3ds max. You can link objects together using the [icon] Select and Link tool on the main toolbar.

Unlike attaching or grouping, linking allows the objects to move or rotate somewhat independently of one another. One way to understand the difference is to envision a stack of spools. If you glue the spools together end to end, you'll end up with a long, rigid stick—this is like attaching or grouping the objects.

But if you loosely thread a piece of string through the spools instead, you'll end up with a flexible, whip-like object. Each spool can rotate independently of the others—this is like linking.

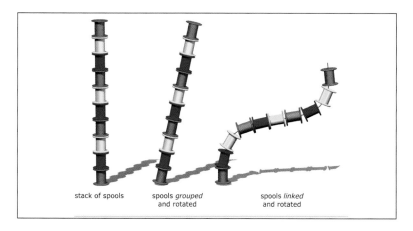

stack of spools   spools *grouped* and rotated   spools *linked* and rotated

The relationship between linked objects is called a *parent-child relationship*. You link the *child* to the *parent*. In the illustration, box 1 is a parent to box 2, while box 3 is a child of box 2.

To link objects with 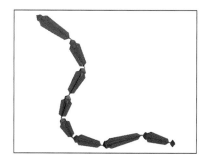 Select and Link, you drag from the child to the parent.

Bones

A *bone* is a special type of object in 3ds max. When you create a series of bones, they're automatically linked together. In addition, you can automatically add animation controls to the chain as you create it. You'll use bones to form your character's skeleton and provide the basis for the character rig.

To access the bone creation tools, click the ⚙ **Systems** button on the 🔧 Create panel, and click **Bones**.

You'll learn more about creating bones later in this chapter.

Chains and Hierarchies

A linear series of linked objects is called a *chain*.

You can also link two or more chains together to form a complex linked structure. Such a structure, in which the child of one object is the parent of the next, is called a *hierarchy*.

In every hierarchy, there is one object that is a parent only, and not a child to any other object. This object is called the *root* of the hierarchy. Every hierarchy has only one root.

There are two ways to create a chain or hierarchy in 3ds max:

- Create a series of ordinary objects such as primitives, and use ![icon] **Select and Link** on the main toolbar to link them together.

- Create bones with *Create panel* > ![icon] *System > Bones*.

Kinematics

In the world of 3D animation, the term *kinematics* describes the movement of a linked structure. Depending on the type of kinematics you use, either parent objects control their children, or child objects control their parents.

Forward kinematics

With *forward kinematics* ("FK" for short), when a parent in the chain moves or rotates, the children under it also move or rotate. This was the only method of kinematics available in the early days of computer animation, and it still has many uses.

Inverse kinematics

With *inverse kinematics* ("IK" for short), you can move a child object and the parent objects will rotate accordingly. For example, you could move a character's hand to cause the upper arm and lower arm to move and rotate appropriately.

With IK, the root of the chain can rotate, but it can't move. In the example of the arm and hand, the upper arm is the root of the chain, so it rotates but doesn't move. By contrast, the lower arm can both move and rotate when the hand is moved.

IK is extremely useful for character animation. It takes a bit of work to set it up, but once it's in place, animation is easy and intuitive. In this section, you'll learn how to use both FK and IK on a skeletal structure in 3ds max.

Character Structure

The diagram shows a humanoid skeleton made with five chains:

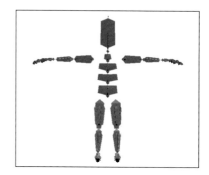

- Spine with head

- Two arms

- Two legs

In this chapter, you'll create five bone chains for your character. In the next chapter, *Rigging the Bones,* you'll link them together with custom control objects.

Bone Creation

To create bones, go to the [icon] **Create** panel and click the [icon] **Systems** button, which is all the way over at the right of the panel. Click **Bones**.

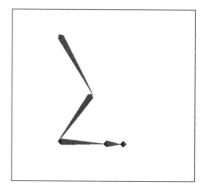

Click in any viewport, then move the cursor and click again. A bone is created between the two points. Continue to move the cursor and click to create more bones. When you've finished creating the chain, right-click to end bone creation.

As you create bones, they are linked in sequence. The first bone you create is the root (parent of all bones). The next is the child of the root, the one after that is the child of the root's child, and so on down the line until you create the last child.

You can move the entire chain by moving the root bone. You can also move the chain by selecting all the bones and moving them all at once. Moving individual bones other than the root moves some of the bones, but not all of them.

A number of options are available on the Create panel for bones. For example, you can automatically assign IK controls to the bones as you create them by checking **Assign to Children** on the IK Chain Assignment rollout before you create the bones. This option is useful if you're creating one chain to control a simple structure, but not necessarily useful for the complex hierarchy required for character animation.

In the exercises in this book, you won't assign IK controls automatically as you create bones. You'll learn more about IK chains later, when you create them manually for your bone structure.

After you create the bones, you can go to the 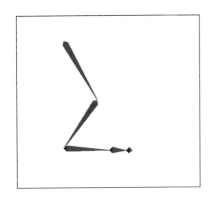 Modify panel and change the Bone Parameters. These parameters change the width of the selected bone, and allow you to add fins. *Fins* are simply extrusions from the bone that help you visualize the bone's placement, and can help with the skinning process later on.

By default, bones don't render in the scene. You can make them render by selecting all the bones, choosing *Edit > Object Properties,* and checking the *Renderable* checkbox on the Object Properties dialog.

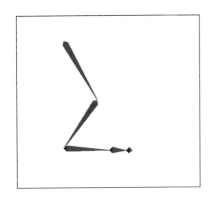

PRACTICE G

Creating a Bone Structure

In this exercise, you'll practice creating bones. The goal is to create a leg bone structure similar to the one shown.

Create One Leg

To create bones, click once to start the leg structure, then click at each joint to set the bone. When you've finished, right-click to end the process.

1. Reset 3ds max by choosing *File > Reset.* Answer **Yes** when asked if you want to reset.

2. On the **Create** panel, click the  **Systems** button.

3. Click **Bones**.

4. In the IK Chain Assignment rollout, make sure **Assign to Children** is unchecked.

5. In the Left viewport, click near the top left of the viewport, then move the cursor down and slightly to the right, and click again.

    You have just created the thigh bone. You will be clicking continuously until the entire bone chain has been created.

6. Move the cursor down and to the left, and click again to create the lower leg.

7. Move the cursor to the right to begin the foot bone, and click again.

8. Move the cursor farther to the right to create the toe bone, and click again.

9. Right-click to end the bone creation process.

    The last click creates a small nub at the end of the toe. This small bone is necessary for character rigging.

    If you had difficulty creating the leg structure, delete the bones and try again. Keep practicing until you can easily create bone structures.

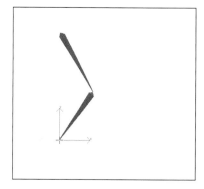

Adjust the Bones

1. Use  **Select and Move** to move different bones around. Note the following:

    ■ Moving the root moves the entire structure.

    ■ Moving a child causes its children to move with it, and causes its immediate parent to rotate.

    ■ The bones never change length, even when moved.

2. Select any bone and go to the ![Modify icon] **Modify** panel.

3. Adjust various parameters on the panel, and observe the results.

   Turning on any of the fin options creates extrusions from the sides of the bones. The fins can help you visualize the thickness of the mesh during the animation process.

Create a Hierarchy

You can make a hierarchy by creating a new chain of bones off an existing chain.

1. On the Create panel, click **Bones** again.

2. Click an existing bone, and start creating another chain.

   This will create a new chain off the first one, creating a hierarchy of two chains.

3. You can save this scene if you like, but it isn't necessary.

Bone Tools

After you've created a bone structure, you might find you need to change the length of one or more of the bones. You can do this with Bone Tools.

Choose *Character > Bone Tools*. The Bone Tools dialog appears.

There are many things you can do with bones in this dialog. For now, we'll focus on changing the length of a bone.

In the Bone Tools dialog, click **Bone Edit Mode**. Select a bone in the middle of the chain, and use **Select and Move** to move it around.

As you move the bone, it becomes longer or shorter, and its parent changes length accordingly. Compare this with moving the bone when Bone Edit Mode is turned off, which rotates the bone but does not change its length.

When Bone Edit Mode is on, the root and last child bones behave a little differently from the others. The root becomes longer or shorter but doesn't affect its parent, since it doesn't have one. The last child object, the nub at the end of the chain, doesn't change in length as you move it. It does, however, affect the length of its parent bone.

On the Bone Tools dialog, you can also create or adjust fins for several bones at once on the Fin Adjustment Tools rollout.

Editing Bones with Bone Tools

For this practice, you can use the bones you created earlier, or create a new chain.

1. Choose *Character > Bone Tools*.

2. In the Bone Tools dialog, turn on **Bone Edit Mode**.

3. Practice using **Select and Move** to change the lengths of bones to understand how this tool works.

4. Click **Bone Edit Mode** again to turn it off.

5. Expand the Fin Adjustment Tools rollout.

6. Select several bones. Change the fin options and observe the result.

   Be sure to turn on **Side Fins**, **Front Fin**, or **Back Fin** to make the fins appear.

7. In the Bone Objects group, change the **Width** and **Height** parameters. Observe the result.

   The **Width** and **Height** parameters change the bone's dimensions without changing its length.

8. Change the **Taper** parameter and observe the result.

   The **Taper** parameter affects the degree to which the bone narrows from the parent end to the child end.

9. You can save this scene if you like, but it isn't necessary.

Where Do You Put the Bones?

In the next tutorial, you'll begin to create the bones for the character. Ideally, you should place each set of bones right at the center of the corresponding part of the model. For example, the bones for the right leg should run down the center of the character's right leg and foot. The bones for the spine should be placed at the center of the character's torso.

After you create bones, you can adjust them and move them around if necessary. This takes a little time, but it's well worth it in the end. Well-placed bones make it easy to apply the Skin modifier and animate the character, while badly placed bones turn the animation process into a nightmare. If you try to fix the bones after applying Skin, you'll make a mess of your character mesh.

TUTORIAL R1

Creating the Leg Bones

In this exercise, you'll create a bone structure for your character. If you haven't done so already, create a folder on your hard disk named *Rigs* to hold your character rig files.

The rigging exercises shown here create a rig for the *Skater_Char.max* character from the *Models* folder on the CD. If you like, you can use the character you created in the previous section of this book. If this is your first time creating a character rig, I strongly recommend that you use a simple humanoid character, and not an alien, monster, or animal. Later, after you've gone through the process once, you can apply what you've learned to a more complicated character.

At any point during this exercise, you can load the rigging file from the CD to see how it's done. For example, if the exercise tells you to save the file *CharRig12.max*, you can load this file from the CD as an example.

Prepare the Character for Rigging

1. Load the the character you created earlier in this book, or load the file *Skater_Char.max* from the CD.

   Important: If you're using your own model, make sure the character is facing the Front viewport, and rotate it if necessary. Otherwise, some of the steps in this tutorial might not work as expected.

2. If any parts of the character have a TurboSmooth modifier applied to them, remove the modifier. To do this, select the object, go to the **Modify** panel, highlight *TurboSmooth* on the stack, and click [🔒] **Remove modifier from the stack**. Alternatively, you can click the light bulb next to TurboSmooth in the stack to turn it off.

   The character might look a little strange without smoothing, but it will be much easier for you to rig the character this way. You can reapply it later, after the rig is done.

3. Select all parts of the character.

4. Create a Named Selection Set and give it the name **Mesh** in the **Named Selection Set** area on the main toolbar.

   The term *mesh* is another name for a model. In a 3D scene, the named selection set *Mesh* will distinguish the model from other objects in the scene, such as bones and rig controls.

5. When you perform the rigging tasks, your job will be much easier if the character is aligned with the construction grid. In the Front viewport, press the **[G]** key to display the construction grid, if it isn't already displayed. Move the character so it's standing on the construction grid.

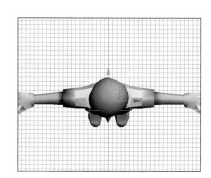

6. In the Top viewport, turn on the grid if necessary, and move the character in any viewport so it's centered on the Y axis.

   If you prefer to work with the grid turned off, you can turn it off with the **[G]** key after you've finished aligning the character with the construction plane.

7. It will also be easier to set up the rig if you make the character see-through. Press **[Alt-X]** on the keyboard to make the character see-through.

8. To freeze the character, right-click in any viewport and choose *Quad > Freeze Selection*.

9. If you like, change the display for each viewport to a shaded view. To do this, right-click the viewport label and choose *Smooth + Highlights* from the pop-up menu.

Create the First Leg Structure

1. In the Left viewport, zoom in on the character's legs.

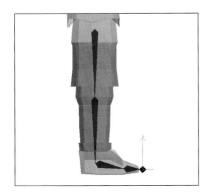

2. In the **Create** panel choose 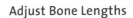 *Systems > Bones*.

3. In the IK Chain Assignment rollout, make sure **Assign to Children** is unchecked.

4. Starting near the character's hip, create a bone structure for the leg with thigh, calf, foot, and toe. The click for the end of the toe should be right at the tip of the character's foot. Right-click to end bone creation.

   Don't be concerned if your leg bones aren't exactly right for your character's legs, or if they don't match the picture exactly.

Adjust Bone Lengths

Look at the leg bones only in the Left viewport for now. If the leg bones match the character's leg when viewed in the Left viewport, and if the nub sticks out past the end of the foot, you can skip this set of steps.

1. Choose *Character > Bone Tools*.

2. In the Bone Tools dialog, click **Bone Edit Mode**.

3. In the Left viewport, adjust the lengths and positions of the leg bones until they fit inside the character's leg.

4. Move the toe nub so it begins at the tip of the character's foot.

5. Turn off **Bone Edit Mode**.

Move the Leg Bones

Now that the bones match the character in the Left viewport, you can work on matching them in the Front viewport.

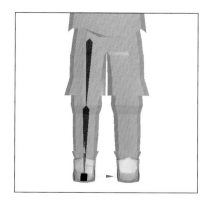

1. In the Front viewport, move the root bone (thigh bone) so the top of it sits at the center of the character's right hip. Don't look at the rest of the bones—work with just the top of the thigh for now. Zoom in to the viewport, if necessary, to get the placement just right.

2. Move the calf bone so the knee joint matches the character's right knee.

3. If this makes the thigh bone so short that it doesn't reach the knee area, choose *Character > Bone Tools* and turn on **Bone Edit Mode**, then move the calf bone downward to make the thigh bone longer. Turn off **Bone Edit Mode** when you're done. You can leave the Bone Tools dialog open while you continue, as long as Bone Edit Mode is turned off while you're moving the bones into place.

4. In the Left viewport, select the foot bone.

5. In the Front viewport, move the foot bone until the calf bone goes down the center of the character's right calf.

6. If this makes the calf bone too short, use **Bone Edit Mode** to move the foot bone into the character's foot, which will lengthen the calf.

7. Check the placement of the bones in all viewports, and make any necessary adjustments.

    Study the relationship between the bones and the character carefully in both the Front and Left viewports. Make sure the bones run down the center of the leg and foot before continuing.

Name the Leg Bones

Naming objects and bones properly is a very important part of character rigging. If you don't name your bones, your scene will become confusing to you later on. For some reason, no one likes to take the time to name the objects in their scene. This step will take less than two minutes, but will save you a lot of time and frustration later on.

1. Name the bones as follows, starting from the root:

   - BoneThighR
   - BoneCalfR
   - BoneFootR
   - BoneToeR
   - BoneToeNubR

2. Save the scene in your *Rigs* folder with the filename **CharRig01.max**.

TUTORIAL R2

Finishing the Leg Bones

Create Fins

During the animation process, you'll probably have the character mesh hidden, and you'll only be able to see the bones. In this case, fins can be very handy for helping you visualize the character's dimensions.

The goal in creating fins is to increase the width of the bone until the fins fill up about three-fourths of the character mesh at that point. Adjusting fins is not an exact science; it's far more important to center the bones on the mesh than it is to make the fins a particular size.

1. Select all the bones except the toe nub.

2. If the Bone Tools dialog isn't already open, choose *Character > Bone Tools*.

3. Check the **Side Fins**, **Front Fin**, and **Back Fin** options.

   This creates fins with the default size of 5.

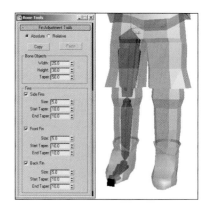

4. Select the thigh bone only.

5. In the Bone Objects group of the Bone Tools dialog, change the parameters to the following:

Width	25
Height	30
Taper	50

   The bone should fill out approximately three-fourths of the character mesh at each part, so these fins will be sufficient for the character's thigh. If you are rigging your own character, you might have to adjust these fin settings to fit the mesh.

6. Select each bone in turn, except the toe nub, and adjust the **Width**, **Height**, and **Taper** values for each, so each bone fills about three-fourths of the mesh around it.

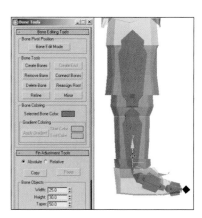

7. Save the scene in your *Rigs* folder with the filename **CharRig02.max**.

   You can quickly save the file with this name by choosing *File > Save As* and clicking [+].

Mirror the Leg Bones

Now that you have one leg set up correctly, you can mirror the leg bones to the other side of the character's body. To do this, you'll use the Mirror tool on the Bone Tools dialog.

Using the Mirror tool on the main toolbar actually scales an object by –100%. This negative scaling can cause problems if the bones are exported to a game engine. This is why we'll use the Mirror tool on the Bone Tools dialog to mirror the bones without this negative scaling.

1. In the Front viewport, select all the leg bones.

2. In the Bone Tools dialog, click **Mirror**.

   The Bone Mirror dialog appears. This dialog works similarly to the Mirror dialog for ordinary 3ds max objects.

3. In the Bone Mirror dialog, make sure **X** is selected as the **Mirror Axis**, and increase the **Offset** to about **50** to move the new bone set to the character's left side. Click **OK**.

   You might also have to move the new leg bones manually to get them into the right positions.

4. Change the names of the new bones to **BoneThighL**, **BoneCalfL**, **BoneFootL**, **BoneToeL**, and **BoneToeNubL**.

5. Save your scene as **CharRig03.max**.

TUTORIAL R3

Creating the Spine Bones

Next, you'll create the spine bones, which will go right up into the neck and head. The logical thing would be to create them up the center of the character's back, but this can cause a problem. When you click near the base of the spine, the new bones will try to attach themselves to the thigh bones. We want the spine to remain separate, and then we'll rig it to the legs later.

To do this, you'll create the bones just behind the character's back, away from the existing bones, then move the spine bones into place.

Create the Bones

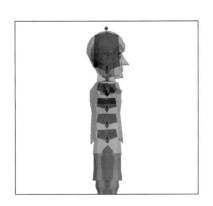

1. Load the file *CharRig03.max* you created earlier, or from the CD.

2. On the **Create** panel, choose 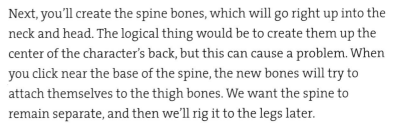 *Systems > Bones*.

3. In the Left viewport, create six bones up the character's back. Start behind the hips and work upward, creating four bones for the back, one for the neck, and one for the head, as shown. Right-click to create the nub and end bone creation.

4. In the Left and Front viewports, move the bone at the base of the spine to the center of the character's hips.

Finish the Bones

1. Choose *Character > Bone Tools*. For each spine bone, adjust fins to make each bone fill about three-fourths of the character mesh. You can select all the spine bones, and adjust the fins for all of them at once. Close the Bone Tools dialog when you have finished.

2. Name the spine bones as follows, starting from the lowest spine bone:

    - BoneSpine01
    - BoneSpine02
    - BoneSpine03
    - BoneSpine04
    - BoneNeck
    - BoneHead
    - BoneHeadnub

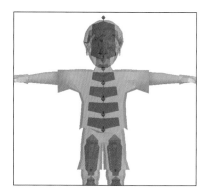

3. Save the scene as **CharRig04.max**.

TUTORIAL R4

Creating Arm and Hand Bones

The arm bones require several parts: a clavicle, the arm bones, and several bones for the fingers.

The *clavicle* is your collarbone, which controls the shoulder's rotation. You'll use the character's clavicle to animate the shoulders when its arm moves up or down a great deal. This bone might seem unimportant, but leaving it out would make the resulting animation look stiff and unnatural around the shoulders.

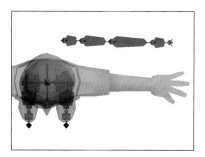

Create the Arm Bones

1. Continue with the scene you just used, or load the file *CharRig04.max* from the *Rigs* folder on the CD.

2. Go to *Create >* [icon] *Systems*, and click **Bones**.

3. Turn on **Side Fins**, **Front Fin**, and **Back Fin**.

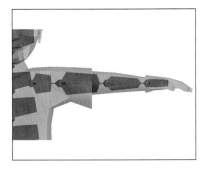

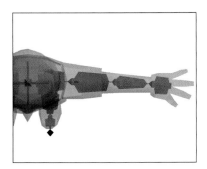

With these options turned on, the bones will be created with fins automatically.

4. In the Top viewport, create five bones and a nub. Start at the neck area and create a clavicle, then create an upper arm bone, a lower arm bone, and a palm bone. Right-click to end bone creation and create a nub at the end of the chain.

5. In the Top and Front viewports, move the upper arm bone to move the entire arm structure to sit inside the character's arm.

6. Choose *Character > Bone Tools*. Use **Bone Edit Mode** to adjust the lengths of the bones, and adjust the fin sizes as necessary. Check your work in the Front and Left viewports. Be sure to turn off **Bone Edit Mode** when you have finished.

7. The nub at the end of the chain allowed you to create a palm bone and easily adjust its length by moving the nub. But you won't need it for the rig, and it will only get in the way, so delete it now.

8. Name the bones as follows:

    ■ BoneClavicleL

    ■ BoneUpperArmL

    ■ BoneLowerArmL

    ■ BonePalmL

Create the Finger Bones

Next you'll create finger bones and link them to the palm bone.

1. In the Top viewport, zoom in on the left hand.

2. Go to *Create > ⚙ Systems*, and click **Bones**. Turn off the fin options for all the bones.

3. In the Top viewport, create the bones for the pinky. Move the cursor to the base of the pinky finger, then click to set the first bone. Click twice more to create the bones along the finger, then right-click to end bone creation and create the finger nub.

Take care not to link the pinky to the palm bone as you create the new bone structure. If you do so, the bone will begin at the center of the hand. If this happens, undo bone creation and try again. If the bones don't fit inside the fingers, you can adjust the bones' sizes. To do this, adjust the Width and Height parameters in the Bone Objects group on the Bone Tools dialog.

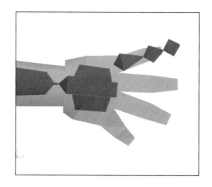

4. Create similar chains for the middle finger and index finger.

If the finger bones try to connect to the palm upon creation, try creating the bone structure away from the hand and moving it into place afterward by moving the base finger bone.

5. Create the bone structure for the thumb.

Note that the base thumb bone begins halfway down the hand. If you look at your own thumb bone, you will see that its rotation actually begins close to the wrist. Placing the bone in this way will make it possible to animate the thumb more realistically.

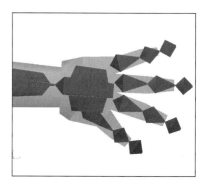

6. If necessary, move the bones in the Front viewport so they sit inside the character's hand.

If you look at the finger bones in the Front viewport, you'll see that they go straight ahead while the character's fingers bend. You'll make the finger bones bend to match the character's fingers when you set up the finger controls in the next chapter.

7. Name the finger bones as shown in the illustration.

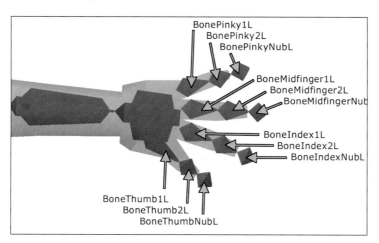

This might seem like a lot of bones to name. But it will only take 5–10 minutes, and the names will help you a great deal when you set up the rig for the fingers.

8. Link each of the finger base bones (the bones with the suffix 1L) to the palm bone.

9. Save the scene as **CharRig05.max**.

Mirror the Arm

This procedure takes just a few minutes, and it will enable you to see the entire bone structure and its relationship to the mesh. It will also give you practice in renaming objects.

1. Select all bones of the arm and hand, including the clavicle and fingers.

2. In the Bone Tools dialog, click **Mirror**.

3. In the Bone Mirror dialog, change the **Offset** to move the arm to the correct position on the left side of the body, and click **OK**.

4. Check the alignment of the finger bones in the Top viewport. If the character is not perfectly symmetrical, you might have to adjust the arm or finger bones to make them fit properly.

5. Change the names of the right hand bones to the same as those for the left, but with an R on the end instead of an L.

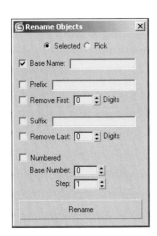

To quickly rename all the objects, press [H] on the keyboard to display a list of the objects in the scene, and type *L01 in the field at the top of the Select Objects dialog to display all the newly copied bones. Click **Select** to select them. Then choose *Tools > Rename Objects*. In the Rename Objects dialog, choose **Selected**. Turn on **Suffix** and **Remove Last**, and turn off all other options. Enter R for **Suffix**, and set the **Remove Last** number to 3. Click **Rename** once, and close the dialog. The bones will be renamed with the letter R instead of L01.

If you want to see how the structure is now linked, press the [H] key to open the Select Objects dialog, and check **Display Subtree** at the bottom of the dialog. Child bones are displayed as indented below their parent objects.

6. Select all the bones, and create a named selection set called **Bones**.

7. Save the scene as **CharRigo6.max**.

The bone structure is complete. Now you can get on to the task of setting up controls for the rig.

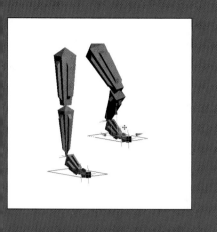

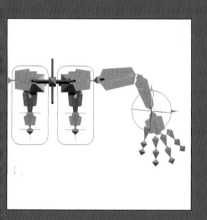

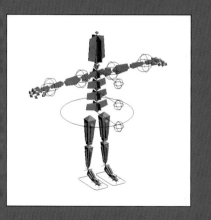

CHAPTER 4

Rigging the Bones

A rig is constructed from bones and other objects and parameters. Your character has a skeleton now, but there's still no really easy way for an animator to move it around. In this chapter, we'll add the controls that make animation a breeze.

For example, you'll create a shape that controls foot motions, including a foot roll for a walking motion. You'll also create custom parameters to make the fingers curl, and a number of other objects and parameters to control the character in every way necessary.

Terms and Concepts

If you're new to rigging, you may find some of the concepts a little difficult to grasp until you actually try them out. To start out, though, you still need a basic understanding of a few terms.

Coordinate Systems

When you move, rotate, or scale an object, you use a set of XYZ axes that appear in the viewports. The directions in which these axes point represent the current *reference coordinate system,* which is simply a method of referring to locations and directions in 3D space. These axes exist solely to make it easier for you to *transform* (move, rotate, scale) the objects in your scene.

In 3ds max, a number of coordinate systems are available for you to use at any time. Each one has a different way of determining which way the selected objects' axes will point. Changing the coordinate system doesn't change the objects in the scene in any way—it simply changes the axes displayed when you select an object.

By default, the reference coordinate system is set to the *View* method. This method orients the XYZ axes depending on the active viewport. The X and Y axes are always perpendicular to the active viewport, except in Perspective or User viewports.

You can see the available coordinate systems on the *Reference Coordinate System* drop-down menu, which is located just to the right of the Select and Uniform Scale button on the main toolbar.

> ▶TIP◀
>
> The place where the X, Y, and Z axes meet is referred to as the axes' *origin point*, or *0,0,0 point*.

> ▶TIP◀
>
> Each transform can have its own reference coordinate system. When you select a coordinate system, it is selected for the current transform only.

Local Axes

When you create an object, 3ds max assigns it a set of *local coordinates* or *local axes*. These axes rotate with the object.

To see an object's local axes, rotate it slightly, click **Select and Move**, and choose Local as the Reference Coordinate System. The directions of the local axes appear in viewports.

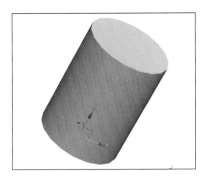

IK Chains

Recall that inverse kinematics (IK) allows you to control an entire chain by moving a child in the chain. For example, you'll be able to control the thigh and calf by moving one IK chain at the heel. An *IK chain* is a control object that allows you to manipulate bones with the IK method.

The IK chain is created as an object called **IK Chain01** that appears as a set of crosshairs and a line connecting the starting and ending bones. You can select an IK chain like any other object by clicking the crosshairs, but the IK chain doesn't render.

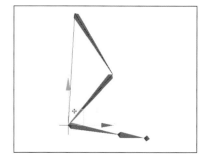

An IK chain has special properties. When you select an IK chain, the crosshairs are the part that's really selected. The line that appears between the starting and ending bones is just a reference, so you can see where the chain starts and ends.

The IK chain isn't "linked" to the bones in the usual sense of linking, nor are the bones linked to the IK chain. The movement of the bones, however, depends on the animation of the IK chain.

You can create an IK chain by selecting the first bone you want to use in the chain, choosing *Animation > IK Solvers > HI Solver,* then clicking the last bone for the chain.

An IK chain is different from any other object in 3ds max. It's not like a box or a sphere, or even like bones. If you select an IK chain and go to the Modify panel, there's nothing there to modify. All the controls for an IK chain are on the Motion panel.

PRACTICE 1

Creating an IK Chain

1. Reset 3ds max.

2. Create a quick set of leg bones to use for practice.

3. Select the root of the chain, which is the thigh bone in this case.

4. Choose *Animation > IK Solver > HI Solver,* then click the foot bone.

Just before you click, a dotted line appears from the thigh to the foot. After you click, the IK chain is created. You can see it as a line extending from the top of the thigh to the heel, and a set of crosshairs at the heel.

5. Use 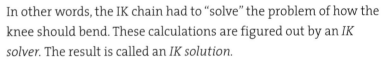 **Select and Move** to move the crosshairs. The foot moves with the crosshairs, and the knee bends to accommodate the motion.

6. Turn on **Auto Key**, and set keys for the crosshairs on different frames.

   Fun, isn't it? You could probably spend all day playing with this one leg. But there are more adventures in store, so let's move along.

7. Save your work as **Practice_IkChain01.max**.

Now that you have an idea of how an IK chain works, let's go over a few more of the concepts that go with it.

IK Solvers

When you moved the IK chain's crosshairs around, 3ds max actually moved the foot first, then calculated how the thigh and calf should rotate to accommodate the movement. It had to decide whether to bend the knee forward, backward, or sideways, and it had to figure out by how much to bend the knee to make the foot go where you placed it.

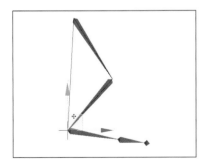

In other words, the IK chain had to "solve" the problem of how the knee should bend. These calculations are figured out by an *IK solver*. The result is called an *IK solution*.

The IK chain's crosshairs represent a *goal* for the IK solution. When you move the goal, 3ds max comes up with a solution for how to move the chain of bones so the end of the last bone in the IK chain can meet the goal.

The HI Solver

Recall that you set up the IK chain by choosing *Animation > IK Solver > HI Solver*. "IK solver" is a general name for the different types of IK chains you can set up and use.

The HI (history-independent) solver is the type of IK solver you'll use in this book. You can find a detailed explanation of its history and usage in the 3ds max documentation, accessible from the *Help* menu. Here, I'll simply state that it's the most versatile and useful one for character animation.

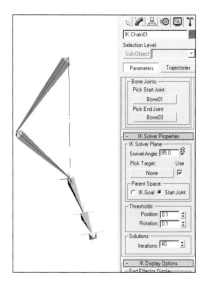

Part of the IK solution involves figuring out which way the bend will point. If you create the bones in a "bent" state, the HI solver will consider that the default bending direction. However, you can make the bend point in a different direction by changing the IK solver's *swivel angle*. To change the swivel angle, select the IK chain and go to the Motion panel. The Swivel Angle parameter is on the IK Solver Properties rollout.

To gain better control over a chain of bones, you can create more than one HI solver on a chain of bones. Multiple HI solvers on a single chain are necessary for most character rigs.

PRACTICE J

Creating Multiple IK Chains

Here, you'll practice creating multiple IK chains on the same bone chain.

Create a Toe IK Chain

1. Load the file *Practice_IkChain01.max* that you created earlier, if it's not still on your screen. You can also load this file from the *Practice* folder on the CD.

2. In the Left viewport, zoom in on the leg structure so you can easily see all the bones.

3. Select the foot bone.

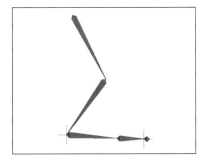

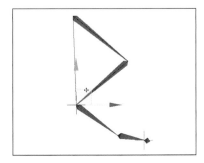

4. Choose *Animation > IK Solvers > HI Solver*, and click the nub at the end of the toe.

Now there are two IK chains on the leg.

Move the IK Chains

1. Use 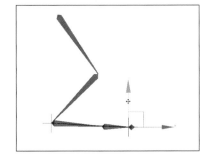 **Select and Move** to select the IK chain at the heel, and move it around.

    The toe stays put while the heel moves. It's OK if the toe bends in the wrong direction—we're just practicing right now.

2. Undo the movement of the heel that you just made.

3. Select the IK chain at the toe, and move it around. The toe moves all by itself.

4. Undo the movement of the toe that you just made.

Make the Entire Foot Move at Once

The way the IK chains are set up now, you'd have to select both IK chains to make the entire foot move at once. However, you can simplify things by linking one IK chain to another, so you only have to move one chain to move the entire foot.

1. Select the heel IK chain.

2. On the main toolbar, click **Select and Link**. Click and drag from the heel IK chain to the toe IK chain.

    The heel IK chain is now linked to the toe IK chain.

3. Select and move the toe IK chain.

    Now the entire foot moves when you move the toe.

4. Undo any movements you just made.

5. Select and move the heel IK chain.

    The heel still moves independently of the toe.

6. Undo any movements you've made before continuing.

Control the Foot Roll

This is a better rig, but it still has a problem. Every time you move the heel, the toe bends or flexes. Animators call this type of bend a *foot roll*, since it's the type of "rolling" action a back foot makes just before coming off the ground to take a step. Foot roll is necessary when you're animating a walk or a run, but only when the foot is about to come off the ground. The foot usually doesn't make this motion when it is in the air.

You can still get some animation out of the rig you've just created, but it would make things unnecessarily difficult. Every time you wanted to raise the heel but not roll the foot, you'd have to be very careful to always keep the heel far enough away from the toe to prevent a mid-air foot roll.

Fortunately, there is a solution. You can prevent unwanted foot roll by adding yet another IK chain.

1. Select the toe IK chain, and delete it.

2. Select the foot bone. Choose *Animation > IK Solvers > HI Solver*, and click the toe bone (not the nub, but the toe itself).

    You might wonder why you're making an IK chain that simply goes from one bone to the next. The answer is, because it makes it easier to control each part of the foot. Let's make another one.

3. Select the toe bone. Choose *Animation > IK Solvers > HI Solver*, and click the toe nub bone.

    If you try moving any of these IK chains, the foot motion won't be very good. You'll need to link them together before you can get any decent results.

    For the purposes of explanation, we'll call the IK chains the heel, middle, and toe IK chains, in that order.

    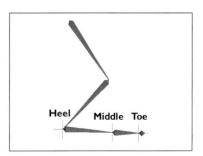

4. Use 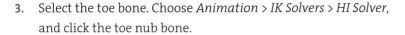 **Select and Link** to link the heel IK chain to the middle IK chain.

5. Link the middle IK chain to the toe IK chain.

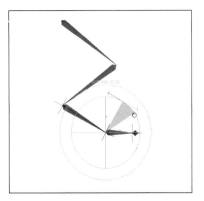

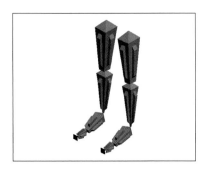

6. Select and move the toe IK chain. The entire foot moves.

7. Select the middle IK chain, and rotate it. The heel comes up off the ground, and the foot rolls only exactly as much as you want it to.

   This is an added bonus of linking IK chains together—you can rotate the child IK chain by rotating the parent.

8. Save the scene as **Practice_IkChain02.max**.

TUTORIAL R5

Creating IK Chains for the Legs

Now you're ready to create the IK chains for your character rig. You'll use the same setup you created in the previous practice exercise.

Load and Hide the Character Mesh

1. Load the file *CharRig06.max* that you created in the previous chapter, or load it from the *Rigs* folder on the CD.

You won't need the mesh for this part of the rigging process, so you can hide it. First you'll have to unfreeze it.

2. Right-click any viewport to display the Quad menu, and choose *Unfreeze All*.

3. From the *Named Selection Sets* drop-down menu, choose the *Mesh* set.

4. Right-click any viewport, and choose *Hide Selection* from the Quad menu.

5. Select and hide all the bones for the upper body, leaving just the legs and feet.

Create the IK Chains

1. If your lower-right viewport displays a Perspective view, change it to a User view. You can do this quickly by activating the Perspective viewport and pressing **[U]** on the keyboard.

2. In the User viewport, use 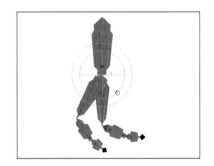 Arc Rotate to adjust the view-port to an angle where you can clearly see and select all the bones in the both legs. Zoom into the viewport if necessary.

3. Select the right calf. In the Left viewport, rotate the calf so it bends like a normal human knee.

   This bend will help the IK chain figure out which way the knee should bend. If you leave the bones straight when you create the IK chain, the knee might bend in any direction.

4. Select the right thigh bone. Choose *Animation > IK Solvers > HI Solver* and click the right foot bone.

5. Use the new IK chain to move the leg back into its original position. You can use the Left viewport to help you match the legs' positions.

6. Create two more IK chains: one from the right foot to the toe, and one from the toe to the nub.

7. Rotate the left calf to bend the knee, and repeat the same steps for the left leg to create three IK chains for that leg.

Name the IK Chains

IK chains can be named like any other object. Simply select the IK chain by clicking the crosshairs, then change the name on the Modify panel.

►TIP◄

Naming IK chains is just as important as naming bones.

1. Go to the Modify panel.

2. Select and rename each IK chain to the names shown in the diagram.

   The middle IK chain is named **IKBallL** or **IKBallR** for the ball of the foot, which is the name for the pad just below the toes.

Link the Chains Together

1. In the User viewport, zoom in on the feet.

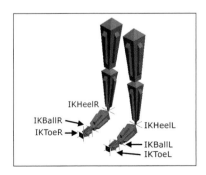

2. For each foot, use 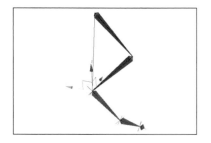 **Select and Link** to link the heel IK chain to the ball IK chain, and the ball IK chain to the toe IK chain. More specifically, link the IK chains together as follows:

   - Link **IKHeelR** to **IKBallR**

   - Link **IKBallR** to **IKToeR**

   - Link **IKHeelL** to **IKBallL**

   - Link **IKBallL** to **IKToeL**

3. To check your linkages, click 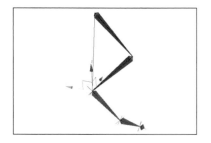 **Select Objects**, then press the [H] key to display the Select Objects dialog. Check the **Display Subtree** checkbox at the bottom of the dialog. The linkages will display with child objects indented beneath their parents.

4. If the linkages appear to be incorrect, select all the IK chains, click 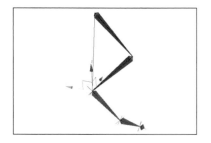 **Unlink Selection** on the main toolbar to remove the linkages, and link them together again.

5. Save the scene as **CharRig07.max**.

►TIP◄

You might wonder why we didn't add the IK chains to just one leg and mirror the entire setup to the other side. This wouldn't work because IK chains don't mirror with the bones mirroring tool. You could use the **Mirror Objects** option on the main toolbar to mirror the bones and IK chains together (if you didn't care about negative scaling), but this doesn't always copy or mirror IK chains reliably. You might end up with a leg bending backward or otherwise behaving strangely.

Customization Tools

Although it now has bones and IK chains, animating your character at this point would still be unweildy. To illustrate this concept, let's consider the character's legs.

To lift the foot and bend the leg, you can move the IK chain at the heel. That's easy, so there's no big problem there.

But suppose you wanted the character to stand on tip-toe. You would have to rotate the foot and toe IK chains individually. Then, if you wanted to swivel the knee outward, you would have to animate the IK chain's swivel angle.

Imagine having to select each of these controls and animate them separately. Now imagine doing this for a long animation. You would quickly become frustrated. And that's just the legs! The problem would be compounded as you animated the spine, head, arms, and fingers.

This is where customization tools come in. *Custom attributes* and *parameter wiring* are two important customization tools that professional riggers use all the time. In this book, you will learn to use them for your character rig.

Custom Attributes

A *custom attribute* is a parameter you can add to any object in the scene. Custom attributes don't do anything on their own, but you can make them control other parameters. Custom attributes are very handy for controlling different parts of a character rig.

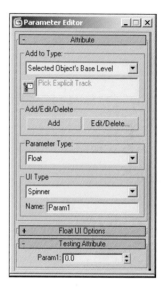

To add a custom attribute to an object, select the object and choose *Animation > Parameter Editor*. The Parameter Editor dialog appears. Here you set the parameter type, name, and range. When you click **Add**, a custom attribute appears on the Modify panel.

A parameter can be added to an object's base level or to a modifier on the stack. Then you can connect the custom attribute to another value used in the character rig.

Shapes

You'll need some extra objects to control the rig, and shapes are an excellent choice. They don't render, so you don't have to remember to hide the controls when you render the animation. In addition, they don't use up as much memory as geometry. This becomes important when you have many characters or objects in a scene. The less memory each character uses up, the faster the screen will refresh.

If you wanted to, you could use helper objects such as Point or Dummy objects to control the character. Like shapes, these objects don't render and use little memory. But for our rig, we'll use shapes only. This will allow us to use the *selection filter* during the animation process, which limits your selection possibilities to one type of object, such as shapes. You'll learn more about the selection filter in the *Animation* section of this book.

►TIP◄

The decision of whether to use shapes, helpers, or primitives to create a character rig is a personal choice a rigger makes. We'll use shapes here, but in your own scenes, you can use whichever object type you prefer.

►TIP◄

When setting up and testing the rig, you'll need to animate it to some degree. If you're unfamiliar with the animation process in 3ds max, or if you just want a refresher, you can read the first part of Chapter 6 (up to the first tutorial) and do the tutorial itself. This will familiarize you with basic animation terms such as *key* and *time slider*.

PRACTICE K

Create a Custom Attribute

In this practice exercise, you'll create a custom attribute and a new object to hold it.

Set up the Scene

1. Open the file *Practice_Gong01.max* from the *Practice* folder on the CD.

   This file contains a simple mechanical version of the gong game found at carnivals. Instead of a person swinging the mallet, the mallet is linked to a swiveling mechanism that allows it to swing down and hit a pad.

   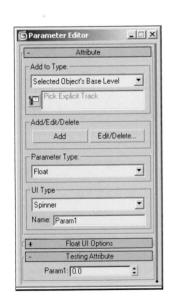

   You'll set up a new custom parameter that will cause the mallet to hit the pad, and make the bell (sphere) rise up the pole. This new parameter has to be associated with an object in the scene, so you'll create a new object to hold the parameter.

2. In the Top viewport, create a small rectangle next to the ground box. Name the rectangle **GongControl**.

Add a Custom Attribute

1. Select the object **GongControl**.

2. Go to the [icon] **Modify** panel.

3. Choose *Animation > Parameter Editor*.

   The Parameter Editor dialog appears.

   The Parameter Type drop-down menu has several options, and the default is **Float**. This simply means a number that can have decimal places. This is what we want for the custom attribute, so leave the Parameter Type set to **Float**. Most other options can also be left at their default values.

4. Change the **Name** to **Ring_the_Gong**.

5. Expand the Float UI Options rollout, and set the **Range** to go from 0 to 200.

6. In the Attribute rollout, click **Add**.

    On the **Modify** panel, you can see the new parameter **Ring_the_Gong** in the new Custom Attributes rollout.

7. Close the Parameter Editor dialog by clicking the **X** at its upper right corner.

    If you change the **Ring_the_Gong** value on the **Modify** panel, nothing happens. That's because the value hasn't been connected to anything yet. Be sure you change the **Ring_the_Gong** parameter back to 0 before continuing.

8. Save the scene as **Practice_Gong02.max**.

► TIP ◄

When you name custom attributes, always use underscores instead of spaces. If you need to use the parameter with advanced tools such as MAXScript and parameter wiring later on, you might run into problems with spaces in parameter names.

Reaction Manager

The Reaction Manager, accessed from the Animation menu, is a new tool in 3ds max 7 that allows you to interactively set up relationships between parameters in a scene. For example, you can use the Reaction Manager to make a custom attribute's value control the X rotation of several objects at once. In other words, once you set up the relationships with the Reaction Manager, you would only have to increase the custom attribute's value to change all those objects' X rotations.

Why use the Reaction Manager, when you could simply rotate the objects? A full character rig has numerous bones and IK chains. While you could animate the skeleton by working directly with the bones or IK chains, this would get tedious after a while. It's far simpler to use the Reaction Manager to set up multiple reactions that will occur when you change a single custom attribute. For example, you will use the Reaction Manager later on to cause the foot bones to roll up naturally just by changing one parameter.

The Reaction Manager works with the concept of one *master* and one or more *slaves,* where the master controls the slaves. For each master, you set up various states for the slaves. For example, the

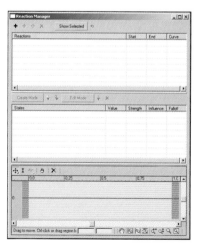

slaves do one thing when the master parameter reaches a value of 50, then they do something else when the master parameter reaches 100.

This might seem confusing at first, but you'll soon find the Reaction Manager to be a very useful tool for character rigging.

Tracks

The Reaction Manager works with *tracks*. A *track* is an animatable parameter associated with an object. For example, a sphere has a Radius parameter that is animatable, so the Radius parameter can also be called a *track*. If you animated the sphere's Radius, you could say you are "animating the sphere's Radius track."

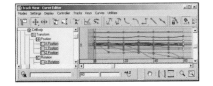

You can easily see an object's tracks by looking at the Track View window (choose *Graph Editors > New Track View*). This window displays all the tracks in the scene over time. In Track View, the tracks are arranged in a hierarchy, which is displayed at the left side of the Track View window. You can click the [+] next to any item in the hierarchy to display its subtracks.

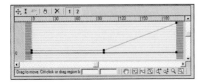

You'll be using Track View later in this book, when you animate the character rig. You don't need to know how to use it right now; I only mentioned it here so you can look at it to get an idea of what tracks are associated with each object.

In addition to its own creation parameters, every object in the scene is assigned a set of default transform tracks. There are separate X, Y, and Z tracks for each of the position, rotation, and scale transforms.

Reaction Curves

▶TIP◀

In 3ds max, all graph lines are referred to as *curves* regardless of whether they are straight or curved.

At the bottom of the Reaction Manager is a graph with lines representing the reactions over time. There is one red line for each slave track.

The numbers across the top of the graph represent master parameter values. The dots mark the states you created for the master parameter. You can use the controls at the bottom right of the graph to zoom and pan the graph.

The slope of the red line indicates how sharply or smoothly the slave parameter will start or stop changing when the master parameter reaches the state values. You can accelerate or decelerate the change by making the lines into curves, and changing the shape of the line.

When setting up reactions, you can sometimes improve the smoothness of the reaction by adjusting its curve. To work with the curves, you can click a key dot to select it, then right-click to change its type from corner to Bezier. Then you can adjust the dot's handles to change the shape of the curve.

PRACTICE L

Setting up a Reaction

In this practice exercise you'll use the Reaction Manager to make the custom attribute control two different parameters in the scene.

1. Choose *Animation > Reaction Manager* to open the Reaction Manager dialog.

    The top pane of the dialog (labeled Reactions) will display the master parameter, and the slave parameters will be listed under it, slightly indented. The bottom pane (labeled States) will display the values for the custom parameters.

2. At the top of the Reaction Manager dialog, click the ➕ **Add Master** button.

3. Click the **GongControl** rectangle. A series of pop-up menus will appear, to guide you through picking one specific parameter associated with this object. Choose *Object (Rectangle) > Custom Attributes > Ring_the_Gong*.

    This places the **Ring_the_Gong** parameter in the master controller listing in the top pane of the Reaction Manager dialog.

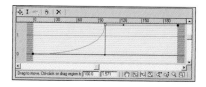

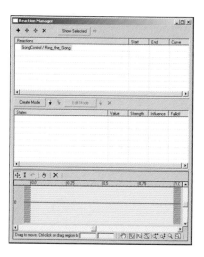

Determine Slave Parameters

Before we can set up the slave parameters, we must figure out what they are. We know the Swivel object will rotate to make the mallet hit the pad, and the bell will go up the pole. But on which axes will these events occur? The slave parameters will be these axes.

To determine the rotation axis for the Swivel object, you'll rotate it appropriately and see which axis is affected.

1. Click ⟳ **Select and Rotate**.

2. Change the coordinate system to **Local**.

3. Select the **Swivel** object, and rotate it so it hits the pad.

    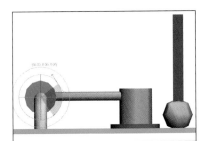

    From the viewport display of the rotation axes, you can see that the local X axis is used to rotate the mallet into place.

4. Undo the rotation.

Now you'll determine the position axis for moving the bell.

5. Click ✛ **Select and Move**.

6. Change the coordinate system to **Local**.

    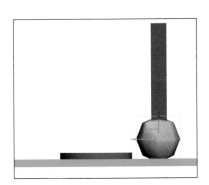

    Even though you just chose the Local coordinate system, it changed back to View when you clicked **Select and Move**. This is because you can have a different coordinate system for each transform. In other words, each time you click a transform button (**Select and Move**, **Select and Rotate**, **Select and Scale**), there can be a different coordinate system in effect.

7. Select the **Bell** object.

    By looking at the transform gizmo on the bell, you can see that the bell would move on its local Z axis to move up the pole.

Set up Slave Parameters

Now that you know which axes will be used as slave parameters, you can set up the slaves.

1. In the Reaction Manager top pane, highlight the master listing **Gong Control/Ring_the_Gong**.

2. Click the ⊕ **Add Slave** button.

3. Click the **Swivel** object. From the pop-up menus that appear, choose *Transform > Rotation > X Rotation*.

    This parameter is added to the Reactions pane in the Reaction Manager, as a slave of the **Ring_the_Gong** master parameter.

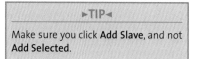

►TIP◄

Make sure you click **Add Slave**, and not **Add Selected**.

4. Click ⊕ **Add Slave** again, and click the **Bell** object. From the pop-up menu, choose *Transform > Position > Z Position*.

    The Reaction Manager now lists both parameters as slaves.

Set up States

The Reacton Manager works with *states*. A state associates a master parameter value with various other parameter values. In this case, we want to create three states: one for the current positions, one for when the mallet hits the pad but the bell hasn't begun to rise, and one for when the bell reaches the top of the pole.

The initial state was already set up when you chose the slave parameters, with the mallet and bell at their rest states and **Ring_the_Gong** set to 0. Now you must set up the other two states.

1. Select the **GongControl** object.

2. On the 🖊 **Modify** panel, increase **Ring_the_Gong** to 100.

3. In the center of the Reaction Manager dialog, click **Create Mode**.

4. Turn on the 🔺 **Angle Snap Toggle**.

5. In the Left viewport, rotate the **Swivel** object so the mallet hits the pad.

6. In the Reaction Manager dialog, click the ⬇ **Create State** button (next to Create Mode).

This creates the second state, where **Ring_the_Gong** is 100 and the mallet is hitting the pad.

7. Select **GongControl** again, and change **Ring_the_Gong** to 200.

8. Move the bell all the way up the pole.

9. Click ⬇ **Create State**.

This creates a third state, where **Ring_the_Gong** is 200, the mallet is hitting the pad, and the bell is all the way up the pole.

10. Turn off **Create Mode**.

Test the Relationship

1. Select **GongControl**.

2. Decrease **Ring_the_Gong** to 100. The ball should descend the pole.

3. Decrease **Ring_the_Gong** to 0. The mallet should return to its original rotation.

If your reactions don't work as expected, go over this practice exercise again until you can get it to work.

Animate the Scene

With the reactions set up, you can easily test how the mallet and ball animate.

1. Turn on **Auto Key**.

2. Move the time slider to frame 30.

3. Set **Ring_the_Gong** to 100.

4. Move the time slider to frame 40.

5. Set **Ring_the_Gong** to 200.

6. Move the time slider to frame 80.

7. Set **Ring_the_Gong** to 0.

8. Play the animation.

    With the reactions set up for the **Ring_the_Gong** parameter, you could animate the mallet ringing the gong numerous times just by setting the parameter.

9. Save the scene as **Practice_Gong03.max**.

►TIP◄

You can also rename the states if you like. To rename a state, click it once in the Reaction Manager, then click again to access the state name. Enter a new state name and press **[Enter]**.

TUTORIAL R6

Creating the Foot Controls

This is the fun part, where you start creating controls for your character rig. You'll create custom attributes and set them up in the Reaction Manager so you can roll the character's feet just by changing parameters on the Modify panel.

Load the Bones Scene

1. Load the file *CharRig07.max* that you created earlier, or load it from the *Rigs* folder on the CD.

Recall that you have already added several IK chains to the character's legs and feet, and that you've linked them together. Let's review the object names.

2. Select a few of the IK chains by clicking on the crosshairs for each one, and look at the name of each one on the **Modify** panel. This will refresh your memory as to how they're named.

3. If you need a refresher on how the IK chains work, you can move or rotate a few of them, then undo what you've done. In particular, remember that you rotate the heel upward by rotating **IKBallL** or **IKBallR** on its local X axis.

Create Control Objects

To simplify the process of animating your character, you'll create a control object for each foot, and add all the foot-related custom attributes to these objects.

1. In the Top viewport, zoom out a little to give you room to place the control objects.

2. In the Top viewport, create a rectangle a little larger than one of the feet. Name the rectangle **CtrlFootL**.

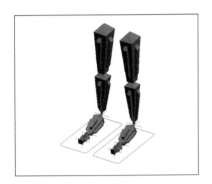

    Be sure to create a rectangle and not a plane. If you like, you can increase the rectangle's **Corner Radius** parameter to give it rounded edges.

3. If necessary, move the rectangle so it sits just under the left foot.

4. Create a copy of the rectangle, and name it **CtrlFootR**. Place this object under the right foot.

5. Select **IKToeL** (the IK chain at the tip of the left foot), and link it to **CtrlFootL**.

Correct the Parent Space

1. To test the rig, go to frame 10, turn on **Auto Key**, and move **CtrlFootL** upward and to the side.

    The entire foot moves with it, as you would expect, but there's a problem. The foot bone spins when you move the foot. You can keep it from spinning by adjusting one of the controls for the IK chain at the ball of the foot.

    You can keep the bones from spinning by changing the *parent space*, or reference point, that the IK chain uses. Right now, it's set to use the **Start Joint** as a reference point, which is at the ankle in this case. Because the ankle changes its rotation when you move **CtrlFootL** up and down, the bones swivel. To solve this problem, you'll use the **IK Goal** setting to keep the bones from spinning when you move CtrlFootL.

2. Turn off **Auto Key**.

3. Select **IKBallL**, the IK chain at the ball of the left foot, and go to the ⊗ **Motion** panel.

4. Locate the IK Solver Properties rollout. In the Parent Space group, select the **IK Goal** option.

   If this causes the bone to turn on its side, change the **Swivel Angle** to –90 or 90 to correct it.

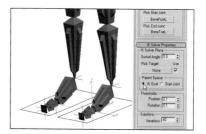

5. Select **IKToeL**, and set its parent space to **IK Goal**. Change the **Swivel Angle** if necessary.

   This will avoid future problems with later parts of the rig causing the bones to spin.

6. Move the time slider to see the foot rise. The bones don't rotate this time.

7. Perform the same tasks on the right foot, linking the IK chains to the control as you did for the left foot. Test the rig by animating **CtrlFootR** on frame 10. Check that the foot moves with the control object, and that the bones don't rotate independently of the foot control.

   Be sure to turn off **Auto Key** when you've finished.

8. Save the scene as **CharRig08.max.**

TUTORIAL R7

Setting up Reactions for the Feet

Now you can add custom attributes and set up reactions to control the feet.

Add Custom Attributes

You'll start with a custom attribute for rolling the left foot. A range of 0 to 90 degrees will work well for this custom attribute.

1. Load the file *CharRig08.max,* or continue from the previous tutorial.

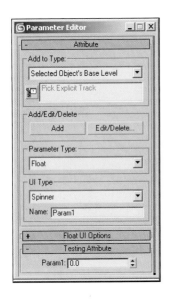

2. Select **CtrlFootL**.

3. Choose *Animation > Parameter Editor*. The Parameter Editor appears.

4. For **Name**, enter **RollL**.

5. On the Float UI Options rollout, change the **Range** to go from 0 to 90.

6. Click **Add**.

   You can see the new parameter on the **Modify** panel, on the Custom Attributes rollout. You don't have to close the Parameter Editor to add the custom attribute to the other foot control.

7. Select **CtrlFootR**, and enter **RollR** as the **Name** on the Parameter Editor. Click **Add** to add the custom attribute to the right foot control.

8. Close the Parameter Editor.

Set up Master and Slaves

Now you'll use the Reaction Manager to set up the reactions for the RollL custom attribute, which will be the master track. You'll need to set the X Rotation tracks for IKBallL and IKToeL as slaves. For IK chains, these tracks are subtracks under *Transform > IK Goal* in the track hierarchy.

1. Choose *Animation > Reaction Manager* to open the Reaction Manager.

2. In the Reaction Manager dialog, click ✚ **Add Master**. Select **CtrlFootL** and from the pop-up menu, choose *Object (Rectangle) > Custom Attributes > RollL*.

3. Because you're wiring the same parameter for two objects, you can choose the slave parameters for both at the same time. Select both **IKBallL** and **IKToeL**.

4. In the Reaction Manager dialog, click **Add Selected**. From the pop-up menu that appears, choose *Transform > IK Goal > Rotation > X Rotation*.

This adds the two X Rotation parameters as slaves. The first state has **RollL** at 0, and both IK chains in their rest positions.

Pin the Stack

Before you set up the reactions, you'll pin the modifier stack so it always shows the **RollL** parameter. This will make it easier to set the foot reactions.

1. Select **CtrlFootL** and access the **Modify** panel.

2. On the **Modify** panel, click **Pin Stack**.

The **RollL** parameter will now show on the **Modify** panel no matter which object is selected in the scene.

Set up Reactions

Now you'll set up two reactions: One when **RollL** is 60, to cause the heel to come off the ground, and another when **RollL** is 90, to have the foot in its fully rolled position.

1. In the Reaction Manager, click **Create Mode**.

2. Increase **RollL** to 60.

3. In the User viewport, rotate **IKBallL** about 45 degrees on the X axis to raise the heel off the ground.

4. Click **Create State**.

5. Change **RollL** to 90.

6. In the User viewport, rotate **IKToeL** on the X axis by about 80 degrees.

Now the foot is very bent over. You'll need to rotate **IKBallL** back to straighten it out.

7. Rotate **IKBallL** by about –70 degrees on the X axis to straighten out the foot.

►TIP◄

To make sure you're selecting the correct objects, you can press the **[H]** key and select them from the Select Objects dialog.

►TIP◄

Using **Add Selected** rather than **Add Slave** allows you to choose the slave parameters for several objects at once. However, this works correctly only if you want to set the same slave parameters for all selected objects. In this case, both slave parameters are the X Rotation track, so Add Selected is fine.

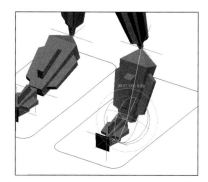

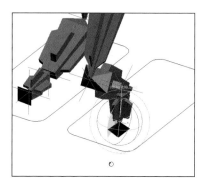

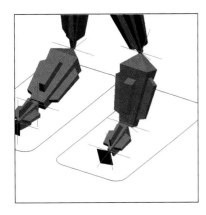

8. Click ⊥ **Create State**.

9. Turn off **Create Mode**.

Now you can test the reactions to see if **RollL** is controlling the foot correctly.

10. Use the **RollL** spinner to decrease its value from 90 down to 0, and back up again.

   If all has gone well, the foot should roll smoothly up and down as you change **RollL**. If it doesn't work, look back over this tutorial to see where you might have gone wrong. If you still can't get it to work, start the tutorial over again.

Set up Reactions for Right Foot

1. On the **Modify** panel, turn off ⊷ **Pin Stack**.

2. In the Reaction Manager dialog, click ➕ **Add Master**, and pick **CtrlFootR**. From the pop-up menu, choose *Object (Rectangle) > Custom Attributes > RollR*.

   When you add this new master track, the Reactions pane will become blank again. You can see the reactions for the left foot again by selecting the **RollL** master track in the Reactions pane. For now, you want to select the **RollR** master track so you can add its slaves.

3. Using the procedure outlined in this tutorial, create slave tracks for the right foot in the same way you did for the left foot.

4. Save the scene as **CharRig09.max**.

Rig Controls

Now that the legs have been rigged, you need some controls for twisting and bending the spine, and for controlling the arms and head. For this, you'll use a few custom shapes aiming for the final result shown. When you rotate and move these shapes, parts of the character's body respond accordingly.

For the legs, you used shapes with custom attributes and reactions. This is appropriate for the feet, where you want them to move through specific poses as they roll up for the walk. You also linked the toe IK chains to the control shapes so you could move the feet around at will.

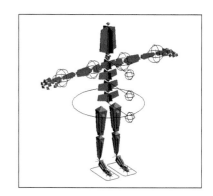

For the rest of the body, the motions are not so predictable. You want to be able to rotate the spine in any direction, and move the hands around as needed. For these controls, reactions aren't appropriate. For example, it wouldn't make sense to set up reactions for every possible arm or spine motion. Instead, you will use other 3ds max mechanisms for controlling the rig.

Pivot Points

In order to continue with the rigging process, you'll have to understand another important animation concept: *pivot points*. An object's pivot point sets the orientation for the local XYZ axes, which determine which way the object rotates on any given axis.

When you create an object—bone, shape, or any other type—in 3ds max, the pivot point and local axes are placed automatically. For bones, the pivot point is placed where you clicked when you started creating the bone, which is the spot between the bone and its parent. For example, the calf bone's pivot point is at the knee, where the thigh and calf bones meet.

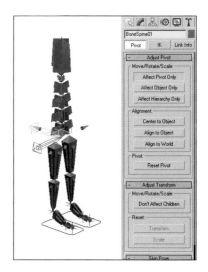

For other objects, 3ds max usually places the pivot point at the center of the object. When you transform an object (move, rotate, scale), the transform gizmo appears at the object's pivot point, and the object transforms in relationship to that point.

When you link one object to another then rotate the parent object, the child rotates around the parent's pivot point. You've already seen this when you linked two IK chains together on the foot. When you rotated the parent IK chain, the child rotated around the parent.

This will also come into play when you set up the spine rig. If you want the spine to rotate along with the control shapes, you'll have to work with pivot points.

You can change an object's pivot point on the 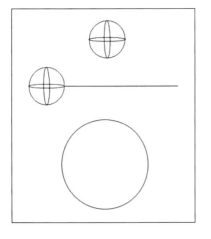 Hierarchy panel. Select the object, click **Affect Pivot Only**, and move or rotate the pivot point.

You can also use the ⬦ **Align** tool when **Affect Pivot Only** is turned on. This is a very efficient way to align one object's pivot point to another's. You'll use this technique often when you rig the spine.

Custom Shapes

There are many custom shapes you can use to rig a character. You've already set up rectangles to control the feet. For the spine and arms, you'll use the following shapes as controls:

- **GYRO** A shape made of three circles. It's used for joints that rotate around all three axes, such as wrists and shoulders. The pivot point can be at its center or elsewhere, depending on what's required for that part of the rig.

- **GYROHANDLE** An alternative version of the gyro that includes a handle. This shape is used to control joints in larger areas of the body, such as the spine. The handle makes the shape easier to select and animate. The pivot point is at the tip of the handle. This means that when you rotate the gyrohandle, the object will rotate around its tip.

- **CIRCLE** A plain old circle. Two or more other controls are linked to it, such as the leg and spine controls. The circle's pivot point is always at the center of the shape.

Spine Motion

When setting up a character rig, you must always think ahead about what types of motion the character will be able to do with

---

►TIP◄

Be sure to turn off Affect Pivot Only when you've finished adjusting the pivot point. Otherwise, you might end up transforming a pivot point when you really intended to transform the object itself.

the rig. There goal here is to use a few simple controls that give you the ability to pose the character in a variety of ways.

To break down the controls, let's take a look at the spine first. What kinds of motions can you make with your own spine? If your back, shoulders, and neck are in good health, you can do the following:

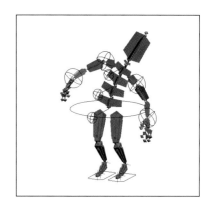

- Bend forward or backward, or from side to side.

- Twist at the shoulders while keeping your hips straight.

- Twist at the hips to turn your entire spine.

- Shake, nod, or tilt your head independently of your shoulders and spine.

Setting up a rig that accommodates all these poses requires a little ingenuity. You won't need IK for the spine; FK will do the trick.

You'll need at least two controls on the spine, plus one for the neck and head. Unless you want to put a control at each joint, you'll also have to get clever with a few other 3ds max concepts, including pivot points and parameter wiring.

Parameter Wiring

Parameter wiring connects, or wires, one value in the scene to another. Parameter wiring is more direct than the Reaction Manager. When you wire two parameters together, there are no states or other delimiters involved. The two parameters influence each other throughout transform animation.

For example, you could wire one object's rotation to the rotation of another object in the scene. When you rotate one object, the other will rotate as well.

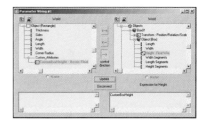

Parameter wiring is particularly useful when straight linking will not accomplish your needs. You'll see this circumstance when you rig the spine.

Parameter wiring is accomplished with the Parameter Wiring dialog. You can open this dialog several ways:

- Choose *Animation > Wire Parameters > Parameter Wire Dialog.*

- Choose *Animation > Wire Parameters > Wire Parameters,* and click the objects and parameters you want to wire.

- Right-click a selected object and choose *Wire Parameters* from the Quad menu, and click the objects and parameters you want to wire.

The use of the custom attributes with parameter wiring is illustrated in the next practice exercise.

PRACTICE M

Wiring a Custom Attribute

In this practice exercise, you'll create a custom attribute for a box, and wire it to the box's height. Then you'll change the box's height using the custom attribute.

Create a Box

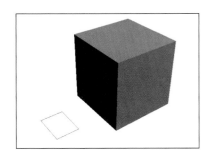

1. Reset 3ds max.

2. In the Top or Perspective viewport, create a box with a **Length**, **Width**, and **Height** of 40 units.

3. On the **Create** panel, click **Shapes**, then click **Rectangle**.

4. In the Top viewport, create a small rectangle, and place it next to the box. Name the rectangle **BoxControl**.

Add a Custom Attribute

1. Select **BoxControl**.

2. Go to the **Modify** panel.

3. Choose *Animation > Parameter Editor.*

   The Parameter Editor appears.

4. Change the **Name** to **CustomBoxHeight**.

5. Expand the Float UI Options rollout, and set the **Range** to go from 0 to 500.

6. Click **Add**.

7. Close the Parameter Editor.

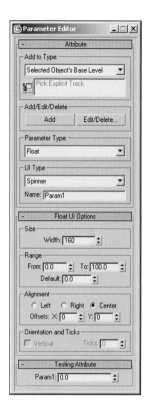

Wire the Custom Attribute

If you change the CustomBoxHeight value on the Modify panel, nothing happens. That's because the value hasn't been wired to anything yet.

1. Right-click **BoxControl**. From the pop-up menu that appears, choose *Wire Parameters > Object (Rectangle) > Custom Attributes > CustomBoxHeight*.

2. Click the box, and from the pop-up menu, choose *Object (Box) > Height*.

   The Parameter Wiring dialog appears, with the tracks you just selected highlighted on either side of the dialog.

3. Now that you've selected the tracks, you need to specify the direction of the wiring. Click the ⟶ right arrow button at the center of the dialog.

   This says that you want the wiring to go from left (the custom attribute) to right (the box's height).

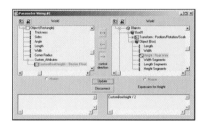

4. Click **Connect**.

   Now the parameters are wired. Don't be concerned when the box becomes completely flat. The custom attribute is currently set to 0, so the box going flat means the wiring is working.

Test the Wiring

1. Close the Parameter Wiring dialog.

2. Select **BoxControl**.

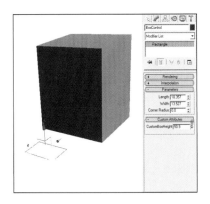

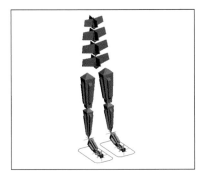

►TIP◄

If you choose to create a gyrohandle yourself, be sure to place the control object's pivot point at the end of the straight portion of the handle. Refer to the 3ds max help (choose *Help > User Reference*) for information on how to move an object's pivot point.

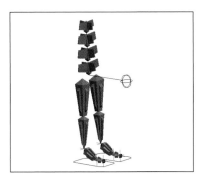

3. On the ⟋ **Modify** panel, increase the **CustomBoxHeight** value.

   If the box's height increases as you increase the **CustomBox-Height** value, the wiring is working properly.

4. Save the scene as **Practice_CA01.max**.

   The "CA" stands for "custom attribute."

TUTORIAL R8

Creating a Spine Control

You'll use gyrohandles to control the spine. You can create your own shapes, or use the ones provided on the CD.

Merge the First Spine Control

1. Load the file *CharRig09.max* that you created earlier, or load this file from the *Rigs* folder on the CD.

2. Unhide the spine bones **BoneSpine01** through **BoneSpine04**. To do this, you can right-click in any viewport and choose *Unhide by Name* from the pop-up menu that appears.

3. Click ⊞ **Zoom Extents All** so you can see the legs and spine.

4. To merge the gyrohandle shape for the scene, choose *File > Merge*. Select the file *ControlShapes.max* from the *Rigs* folder on the CD, and select the object **GyroHandle**.

5. Name the gyrohandle **CtrlSpineBase**. You will use this control shape to rotate the entire spine.

Align and Link the Spine Control

1. Use ⬗ **Align** to align the control shape to the lowest spine bone. In the Align dialog, turn on **Pivot Point** for both the **Current Object** and **Target Object**. Click **OK** to align the objects and close the dialog.

2. Rotate the control object so it sticks out in front of the character.

The gyrohandle will control the entire spine. Since the spine is already linked together, the only thing you need to do to get a basic spine rig is link the bottom spine bone to the control object.

3.  Link **BoneSpine01** to **CtrlSpineBase**.

4. Test the setup by rotating **CtrlSpineBase** on any axis.

   The object rotates from its pivot point, which is positioned at the bottom of the spine. This causes the entire spine to rotate in the same direction you rotated the control shape.

5. Undo any rotation before continuing.

6. Save the scene as **CharRig10.max**.

Set up Double Rotation

Here, you'll wire the rotation of the second-lowest spine bone to the control shape. Then when you rotate the control shape, the bone will receive the rotation twice: Once from the wiring, and once as a child of the bottom spine bone.

As a result, the second-lowest spine bone will rotate twice as much as the lowest one. This will simulate the natural rotation of the spine, where the upper bones rotate more than the lower bones.

1. Select **CtrlSpineBase**.

2. Right-click **CtrlSpineBase** to access the Quad menu, and choose *Wire Parameters*.

3. From the pop-up menu that appears, choose *Transform > Rotation > X Rotation*.

4. Click **BoneSpine02** and choose *Transform > Rotation > X Rotation* from the pop-up menu.

   Because you'll be wiring every axis of the control shape to every axis of the bone, you can save time by wiring the entire **Rotation** listing.

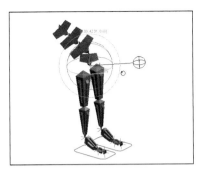

▶TIP◀

There's no need to save the scene since you'll be starting from the last saved file, *CharRig10.max*, when you correct this problem.

5. In the Parameter Wiring dialog, select the **Rotation** listing on each side (the one above X Rotation).

6. Click the ⟶ right arrow and **Connect** to make the Rotation listing on the left control the one on the right, and close the Parameter Wiring dialog.

Woops! The wired spine bone turns in the wrong direction, taking the rest of the spine with it. In addition, if you rotate the control shape, the spine rotates in all kinds of strange directions that have nothing to do with the control shape's rotation. Something's definitely wrong here. Continue on with the next section to find out what went wrong, and how to fix it.

Matching Rotations

Why isn't the spine wiring working? One of the problems is that the control object, and perhaps the spine, have been rotated at one time or another to put them in their current places. The wiring is adding up all the control shape's rotations on whatever its local axes are, and affecting the bone's local axes with this rotation. The chances of this resulting in the expected rotation are pretty slim.

This problem doesn't occur with linking, which is why the bottom spine bone worked fine when you linked it to the control shape. With linking, the child object always follows the parent object's current orientation. This problem is strictly a wiring phenomenon. However, there's no way to get the double rotation effect with linking alone—you have to use wiring for this effect.

You'll get the same result even if you wire individual rotation parameters to one another. For example, wiring the X Rotation of the control shape to the bone's X Rotation parameter won't give you the expected rotation either. You might be able to get some success by doing some cross-wiring, such as wiring the control shape's Z Rotation to the bone's X Rotation, or some variation of this. But you could drive yourself crazy trying to figure out the correct wiring, which might require putting in negative signs and subtracting from 90 or 180 or whatever. Not a fun way to spend your time, and there's an easier way.

Matching Pivot Points

To solve the problem of the mismatched wiring, you want the control shape's local axes to match the bone's. Then any rotation on the control shape will rotate the bone on the same axis. You can solve this problem by aligning the control shape's pivot point to the bone's pivot point. This is an easy task that you can perform with the Align tool.

Freezing Rotations

Although aligning the pivot points will help, it won't solve the problem completely.

If the spine bone was rotated to pose it in place, it had an original orientation when it was created, and now it has its current orientation. You want the spine bone to be affected in relation to its current orientation, not its original orientation. The same goes for the control shape.

For both the spine control and the second-to-last bone, you'll need to *freeze* the rotation in its current state and start any animation from there. Fortunately, 3ds max provides a simple way to do this. You can simply select an object, press **[Alt]** and right-click to display the Animation Quad menu, and choose *Freeze Rotation*.

This splits the Rotation track into two separate tracks named Initial Pose and Keyframe XYZ. The Initial Pose track holds any rotation you've performed up until now to pose the objects. The Keyframe XYZ track will hold the results of any transforming you do from now on.

If you align the pivot points, freeze the rotations, then wire together the Keyframe XYZ tracks, the double-rotation will then work.

Controllers

When you use Freeze Transform, there are some things going on under 3ds max's hood that you should know about.

When you create any object in 3ds max (including bones), it is assigned a single Rotation track by default. This track is a result of a default *controller* being assigned to the object.

A *controller* is a method for specifying an object's transforms (position, rotation, and scale). The default controllers allow you to move, rotate, and scale objects with the transform buttons on the toolbar (Select and Move, Select and Rotate, Select and Scale). Other controllers might control an object's position by putting it on a path, or control its rotation by making it look at another object.

By default, simple controllers are assigned to each of an object's three transforms. If you just went ahead and animated the objects in the scene with the transform buttons and never did any other kind of animation, you might never know the controllers were there. But 3ds max provides additional controllers so you'll have more flexibility when animating.

You can change these controllers in a variety of ways. The most direct method is to select an object, go to the ⊚ Motion panel, expand the Assign Controller rollout, highlight an existing controller, and click the ⟦?⟧ Assign Controller button to choose another controller.

There are also a number of indirect methods for changing controllers in 3ds max. The Freeze Rotation option is one example—it splits the original rotation controller into two controllers. Options in the *Animation > Constraints* menu also change controllers. For example, choosing Path Constraint changes the default position controller to a Path controller.

A *list controller* is a special type of controller that lets you apply two or more controllers to one transform. The first controller holds the current transform information at the time the list

▶TIP◀

In the 3ds max documentation, controllers are also called "animation controllers" or "constraints."

controller is assigned, while later controllers can be used to animate the object. The Freeze Rotation tool automatically creates a list controller for an object.

To save time in changing the default rotation controller to a list controller, you'll use the Freeze Rotation option to set up the double rotation through wiring.

TUTORIAL R9

Completing the Spine Rig

Now you can use what you've learned about freezing rotation to finish setting up the spine rig.

Align the Control Shape's Pivot Point

The first order of business is to align the pivot points of the two objects you want to control with the wiring.

1. Load the file *CharRig10.max* that you created earlier, or from the *Rigs* folder on the CD.

2. Select **CtrlSpineBase**, the gyrohandle that controls the spine.

3. On the 🔠 **Hierarchy** panel, click **Affect Pivot Only**.

4. Click 🔶 **Align**, and click **BoneSpine02**, the second-lowest spine bone.

5. In the Align dialog, turn off any Align Position options that are turned on. In the Align Orientation group, turn on **X, Y,** and **Z**. Make sure **Pivot Point** is selected for both Current Object and Target Object, and click **OK**.

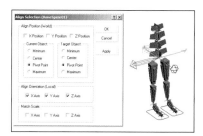

6. Turn off **Affect Pivot Only**.

    Now the orientation of the control object's pivot point matches the pivot point of the bone it's going to control.

Freeze Rotations

1. Make sure **CtrlSpineBase** is still selected.

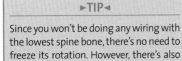

▶TIP◀

Since you won't be doing any wiring with the lowest spine bone, there's no need to freeze its rotation. However, there's also no harm in freezing its rotation.

2. To see what's happening with the Rotation controller, access the ⊛ **Motion** panel. In the Assign Controller rollout, expand the **Rotation** listing.

   The listing currently shows one Euler XYZ controller assigned to the Rotation track. This is the default rotation controller.

3. Press **[Alt]** and right-click, then choose *Freeze Rotation* from the Animation Quad menu.

   In the Assign Controller rollout, if you expand the Rotation controller again, you can see that the Rotation controller has been split into two controllers: Initial Pose and Keyframe XYZ. These are simply EulerXYZ controllers that have been assigned new names. The Initial Pose controller holds the rotation up until this point, while the Keyframe XYZ controller will hold any you do from now on.

4. Select **BoneSpine02**, and apply *Freeze Rotation* to it.

   On the **Motion** panel, you can see that the bone's Rotation tracks are split in the same way.

Wire the Rotation

1. Select **CtrlSpineBase**.

2. Right-click **CtrlSpineBase**, and choose *Wire Parameters* from the Quad menu. Choose *Transform > Rotation > Keyframe XYZ > X Rotation* from the pop-up menu.

3. Click **BoneSpine02**, and choose *Transform > Rotation > Keyframe XYZ > X Rotation*.

   You could wire each of the rotation listings to one another (X Rotation, Y Rotation, Z Rotation), but you can save time by wiring the **Keyframe XYZ** listings together. This automatically wires each of the X, Y, and Z rotation listings to one another.

4. In the Parameter Wiring dialog, highlight the **Keyframe XYZ:Euler XYZ** listing on each side (the one above X Rotation).

5. Click the  right arrow, then click **Connect**.

6. Close the Parameter Wiring dialog.

7. Test the wiring by rotating **CtrlSpineBase**. The second spine bone from the bottom should rotate twice as much as the bottom spine bone when you rotate the gyrohandle in any direction. Undo any rotation before continuing.

8. Save the scene as **CharRig11.max**.

Create the Remaining Spine Controls

The rig for the upper spine and neck works similarly to the rig at the bottom of the spine. Now you know all the tricks, so it's just a matter of setting it up.

1. Unhide **BoneNeck** and **BoneHead**.

2. Create two copies of **CtrlSpineBase**, and name them **CtrlSpineMid** and **CtrlSpineNeck**.

First, you'll align the positions of these new controls to the bones that will link to them.

3. Use 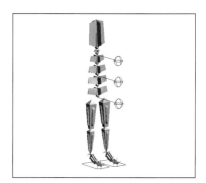 **Align** to align the position of **CtrlSpineNeck** with **BoneNeck**. Set both Current Object and Target Object to **Pivot Point** on the Align dialog.

4. Use **Align** to align the position of **CtrlSpineMid** with **BoneSpine03** (the second spine bone from the top). Be sure to turn off any orientation settings in the Align dialog before clicking **OK**.

Next, you'll change the orientation of each control object's pivot point to match the bone it will control with wiring. The pivot point orientations for all the bones are similar, but to be safe, you should align the pivot points for each set of controls and bones.

5. Select **CtrlSpineNeck**.

6. On the **Hierarchy** panel, turn on **Affect Pivot Only**.

7. 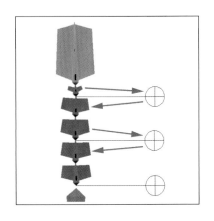 Align the orientation of **CtrlSpineNeck**'s pivot point to **BoneHead**'s pivot point.

    Recall that you aligned the control object pivot point's *position* with the bone that will be linked to it, but you align the pivot point's *orientation* to the bone that will receive the double rotation.

8. Select **CtrlSpineMid**, and align the orientation of **CtrlSpineMid**'s pivot point to **BoneSpine04**'s pivot point.

9. Be sure to turn off **Affect Pivot Only** before continuing.

Link the Controls

Now you can link the bones to the controls. Use the picture as a reference for the link sequence.

1. Link **BoneNeck** to **CtrlSpineNeck**, and link **CtrlSpineNeck** to **BoneSpine04**.

2. Link **BoneSpine03** to **CtrlSpineMid**, and link **CtrlSpineMid** to **BoneSpine02**.

    You now have a linked chain from the top of the head to the bottom of the spine that includes both bones and control objects.

3. Test the linkage by rotating each spine control. The bones above each one, and any controls above each one, should rotate with it.

    Be sure to undo any rotation before continuing.

Wire the Neck and Upper Spine

1. Select **BoneHead**, **BoneSpine04**, **CtrlSpineNeck**, and **CtrlSpineMid**. Press [Alt] and right-click to display the Animation Quad menu, then choose *Freeze Rotation*.

2. Wire the *Keyframe XYZ* controller from **CtrlSpineNeck** to **BoneHead** to create double rotation on the head.

3. Wire the *Keyframe XYZ* controller from **CtrlSpineMid** to **BoneSpine04** to create double rotation on the upper spine.

4. Test the rig by rotating the control objects. You can rotate the entire spine by rotating the control object at the base of the spine, and you can increase the rotation for any joint along the way by rotating its control object.

   Undo any rotation you have done before continuing.

5. Save the scene as **CharRig12.max**.

Tools Review

Let's go do a brief review of the rigging tools you've learned so far.

- **BONES** The objects that make up the skeletal structure.

- **TRANSFORM** Move, rotate, or scale.

- **PIVOT POINT** XYZ axes that set the origin point and direction for transforms.

- **LINKING** Connecting one object to another as parent and child.

- **IK CHAIN** A special control for bone structures that allows transforming the child object to affect the parent object.

- **CUSTOM ATTRIBUTE** A custom-made parameter that you can add to any object.

- **CONTROL OBJECT** A shape or other object that controls part of a rig.

- **TRACK** An animatable parameter.

- **REACTIONS** Connections between tracks, where the master controls the slaves.

- **WIRING** Connecting two tracks in the scene so changing one changes the other.

- **CONTROLLER** A method of specifying how a particular transform will occur. Different controllers make different

►TIP◄

If you link the controls together after you freeze the rotation, you'll have to link the controls together with the Initial Pose controller active in order for the wiring to work properly (rather than linking when the Keyframe XYZ controller is active). To do this, select the control object and, on the Motion panel, double-click the *Initial Pose* controller in the Rotation List rollout to make it the current controller. Link the bones and control together, then double-click the *Keyframe XYZ* controller in the Rotation List rollout to make it the current controller again.

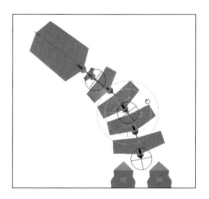

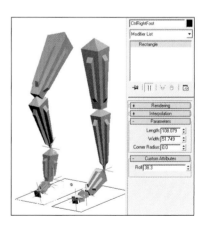

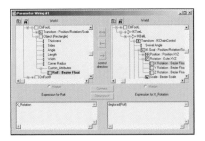

parameters available for animation. Controllers are also called *animation controllers* or *constraints*.

- **LIST CONTROLLER** A special type of controller that lets you apply two or more controllers to one transform. The first controller holds the current transform information at the time the list controller is assigned, while later controllers can be used to animate the object.

- **FREEZE ROTATION** A method of "resetting" the rotation up to the current point so all rotation from this point forward will rotate from the same initial orientation.

Wrist Rig

Let's take a moment to consider what we're going to do with the wrist. You could place a gyro at the wrist, and use it to rotate the hand (palm bone) in any direction. It would also be handy to be able to move the wrist control and have it move the hand and bend the arm.

To make this happen, you can place the gyro at the wrist and link the IK chain to the gyro. So far, so good. But to make the palm rotate with the wrist control, you'd want to link the palm bone to the control object, too.

However, this would create a problem. The palm is part of the IK chain, so you can't link it to another object without breaking the chain. If you break the chain, the arm won't work any more.

To solve this problem, you'll use an *orientation constraint* to make the palm's rotation always match the wrist control. This is a type of controller that forces one object's rotation to always match another's. An orientation constraint is a useful alternative to linking, especially when linking isn't possible.

To make the wrist rotation work intuitively with the orientation constraint, you'll need to align the orientation of the control shape's pivot point with the palm bone's pivot point. There's no need to align the pivot point alone; you can simply align the entire object. This is because a gyro looks the same no matter which way it's oriented.

At this point, you've learned enough to complete the rest of the rig. I'll walk you through the process, but I won't give as much detail in the steps as I did before. Let's see if you can do it!

TUTORIAL R10

Rigging the Wrist

The rig for the hands requires a little more work, but uses principles you've learned already.

Prepare the Scene

1. Load the file *CharRig12.max* that you created earlier, or from the *Rigs* folder on the CD.

2. Unhide all the bones.

3. Hide the spine controls. You won't need them for a while, and they'll only get in the way.

Create the Wrist Control

You'll use an IK solver to rig the upper and lower arms.

1. Select **BoneUpperArmL**, the left upper arm bone. Choose *Animation > IK Solvers > HI Solver*, and click the palm bone to create an HI Solver for the left arm.

2. Name the new IK chain **IKWristL**.

   If you like, you can move the IK chain around a little to ensure the palm is moving along with it. Undo any movements before continuing.

3. Choose *File > Merge*, and open the file *ControlShapes.max* in the *Rigs* folder on the CD. Merge the object **Gyro** from the file.

   This is the shape made from three circles.

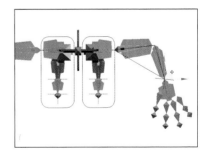

►TIP◄

To quickly unhide all the bones, you can choose the *Bones* selection set that you created earlier. When asked if you want to unhide the objects, answer **Yes**.

4. Name the gyro **CtrlWristL**.

5.  Align the position of **CtrlWristL** with **IKWristL**.

Assign the Orientation Constraint

1.  Align the orientation of **CtrlWristL** to **BonePalmL**.

   This will rotate **CtrlWristL** so its pivot point has the same orientation as **BonePalmL**'s pivot point.

2. Select **BonePalmL**.

3. Choose *Animation > Constraints > Orientation Constraint,* and click **CtrlWristL**.

4. Test the constraint by rotating **CtrlWristL**. The palm should rotate in the same direction as the control shape.

Complete the Wrist Rig

1. Link the IK chain **IKWristL** to **CtrlWristL**.

2. Test the rig by moving **CtrlWristL**.

   The arm and hand should move together, and the elbow should bend. Undo any movements before continuing.

3. Save the scene as **CharRig13.max**.

Fingers and Thumb

Next you'll set up controls to make the fingers and thumb flex and curl. Before you start this process, take a moment to work with your own hand. What are the most common poses you make with your hand, and which fingers do you curl during the poses?

Hand Poses

These are some the most commonly used poses, both in life and in animation:

- **FLEX** Straighten and arch the fingers and thumb back slightly to flatten the hand.

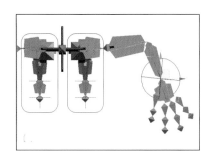

- **NEUTRAL** The hand in a position of rest. This is the way you modeled the character's hand.

- **GRASP** Curl the thumb and fingers partway to hold an object.

- **FIST** Curl the fingers into the palm, and curl the thumb across the fingers.

- **POINT** Curl all fingers into a fist except the index finger.

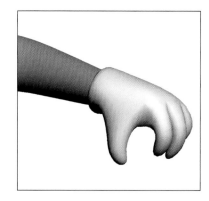

You usually pose your last three fingers the same way, either all curled or all uncurled. For example, it's pretty rare to curl your pinky without curling your second and third fingers. One exception would be curling all your fingers except the middle one to make a gesture that is unacceptable in polite company. Unless you plan to animate your character to make this gesture (and we won't be doing that in this book), you can safely make the last two fingers curl together at all times.

Hand Custom Attributes

To create the hand poses listed above, you can set up three custom attributes:

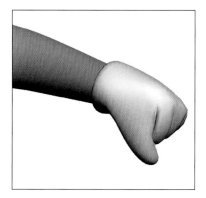

- CurlThumb

- CurlIndexFinger

- CurlTwoFingers

For this rig, you'll use the following values to represent different poses for each custom attribute:

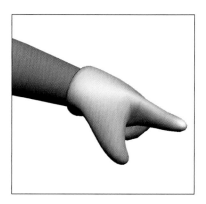

Value	Pose
−20	Flex
0	Neutral
100	Curl partway (as for grasp pose)
200	Curl into palm (as for fist pose)

With each custom attribute set up separately to perform all four poses, you'll be able to make the hand do just about anything a real hand can do.

Why are we using a negative value for the flex pose? Why not just give the flex pose a 0 value, and go up from there? The neutral pose is the pose the bones currently have. When you set up the master and slave tracks in the Reaction Manager, the first state will automatically be set up with the custom attributes at 0 and the fingers in the neutral pose. So it makes sense to give the neutral pose the 0 value.

Because fingers curl toward the palm but flex away from the palm, making the curl poses postive and the flex pose negative will make animation more intuitive.

Rotation Axes

Make the poses with your hand again, and look at the way you rotate your fingers and thumb. Note that each finger joint rotates on only one axis, but the base thumb joint can rotate on any axis. When you set up reactions for the fingers, you'll only need to set up one axis as the slave. For the base thumb joint, you'll need all three axes.

TUTORIAL R11

Rigging the Finger Curls

Here, you'll rig the finger curls by creating custom attributes on the wrist control, then wiring them to the finger rotations.

Determine the Curl Axis

Before we can set up the slave parameters, we need to determine which of the fingers' local axes will be used to create the flexes and curls.

If one finger curls on a particular axis, all the finger bones will use the same axis for curling. This means you only have to test one finger bone to find out the correct axis of rotation for all the fingers.

1. Load the file *CharRig13.max*, if it isn't still on your screen.

2. Zoom in on the hand in the User or Perspective viewport.

3. Click 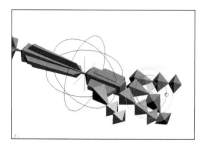 **Select and Rotate**.

4. On the main toolbar, change the **Reference Coordinate System** to *Local*.

5. Rotate one of the fingers in the direction in which it should curl, and watch the number display above the transform gizmo to see which axis changes.

   The number display shows the degree of rotation as [X,Y,Z]. The numerical value will change for only one axis. In the rig included on the CD, the fingers curl on their local Y axes, but it's possible that yours are different.

6. Undo any rotation before continuing.

Create Custom Attributes

You'll use a slightly different method to add the custom attribute to the wrist control. Here, you'll add an Attribute Holder modifier, adding the custom attribute to the modifier level of the stack.

The Attribute Holder doesn't do anything on its own; it simply provides a separate level of the stack just for custom attributes. This modifier is particularly useful when the control object has numerous rollouts at its base level, as an Editable Spline does. By putting the custom attributes on a separate level, you can easily find them when you need to change them.

1. Select **CtrlWristL**.

2. Add the **Attribute Holder** modifier to **CtrlWristL**.

3. Choose *Animation > Parameter Editor*.

4. For the custom attribute **Name**, enter **CurlThumbL**.

5. Enter a **Range** from –20 to 200.

> **►TIP◄**
>
> If you can't see the numerical angle value, choose *Customize > Preferences > Gizmos tab*, and turn on **Angle Data** in the Rotate Gizmo group.

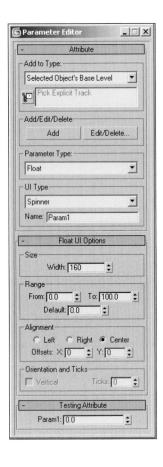

Note that the **Default** value is 0, which will be used for the neutral pose.

6. At the top of the Attribute rollout, make sure that **Add to Type** is set to **Selected Object's Current Modifier**. This will cause the custom attribute to be added to the **Attribute Holder** modifier level of the stack.

7. Click **Add**.

8. Create two more custom attributes with the same ranges, and name them **CurlIndexFingerL** and **CurlTwoFingersL**.

9. Close the Parameter Editor.

   If the custom attributes don't appear automatically on the **Modify** panel, choose the *Editable Spline* level of the stack, then the *Attribute Holder* level again. The custom attributes should appear on the **Modify** panel in a new rollout called Custom Attributes.

Set up Master and Slave for Index Finger

We'll start by setting up reactions for the index finger.

1. Hide all the finger nub objects. This will make it easier to see the finger curls after you set them up.

2. Choose *Animation > Reaction Manager*.

   The master tracks for the two feet are displayed in the Reaction Manager for this scene. You'll add the finger tracks.

3. At the top of the Reaction Manager dialog, click the ➕ **Add Master** button. Click **CtrlWristL**, and choose *Modified Object > Attribute Holder > Custom Attributes > CurlIndexFingerL*.

4. Select the two index finger bones.

5. Click ✛ **Add Selected** on the Reaction Manager dialog, and choose *Transform > Rotation > Y Rotation*.

   This adds the Y Rotation track for both bones as slave tracks, and creates the initial state with all tracks at their default values.

►TIP◄

If your character's fingers curl on the X or Z axis, you should substitute the appropriate axis wherever Y Rotation is mentioned.

Set up Reactions for Index Finger

1. Select **CtrlWristL**.

2. On the **Modify** panel, click ⊞ **Pin Stack**.

3. Change **CurlIndexFingerL** to –20.

4. Click **Create Mode** to turn it on.

5. Rotate the index finger's base (knuckle) bone back by about 10 degrees to flex the finger.

6. Click ▼ **Create State**.

7. Create two more states for the index finger:

    ■ When **CurlIndexFingerL** is 100, rotate the base bone by about 30 degrees, and the second bone by about 70 degrees.

    ■ When **CurlIndexFingerL** is 200, rotate the base bone to curl the finger into the palm until the second bone is almost touching the palm.

8. Turn off **Create Mode** when you've finished.

9. Test the reactions by increasing the **CurlIndexFingerL** parameter to see how it affects the finger. The tip of the finger should nearly touch the palm when **CurlIndexFingerL** is at 200.

    If you like, you can smooth out the curves at the bottom of the graph to see if that improves the motion.

▶TIP◀

You don't have to have Create Mode turned on when you change the master track, only when you change the slave tracks.

Set up Reactions for Remaining Finger Curls

1. In the Reaction Manager, ➕ add the **CurlTwoFingersL** custom attribute as a master track.

2. Use the same process to set up reactions for the **CurlTwoFingersL** custom attribute with the middle and pinky fingers' Y rotation tracks as the slaves. You will have to rotate each finger separately when setting up the reactions.

    If you like, you can change **CurlIndexFingerL** to the same value as **CurlTwoFingersL** while you set up the poses. This can help you visualize how the fingers will work together when flattening the hand and creating a fist pose. Because **CurlIndexFingerL** is not included in the **CurlTwoFingersL** master/slave relationship, changing its value will not affect the reactions.

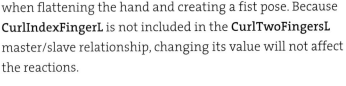

3. Turn off **Create Mode**, and test the rig by increasing **CurlTwoFingers**. The fingers should curl into the palm when **CurlTwoFingersL** reaches 200.

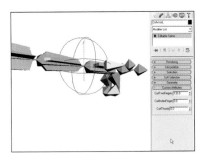

4. Save the scene as **CharRig14.max**.

Set up Thumb Reactions

The thumb rotates a little differently than the fingers. Recall that the base thumb bone can rotate on any axis, so you'll need to add all rotation tracks for this bone as slaves.

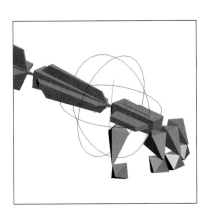

The second thumb bone doesn't rotate in the same direction as the fingers. When you hold your hand flat and rotate just your second thumb bone, you can see that it curls in a direction different from your fingers. Let's test the rig and see which axis this corresponds to.

1. Rotate the second thumb bone slightly toward the palm, and note the axis of rotation. Be sure to undo any rotation before continuing.

   In the rig on the CD, the thumb rotates on the Z axis.

2. In the Reaction Manager, 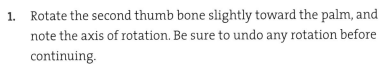 add **CurlThumbL** as a master track.

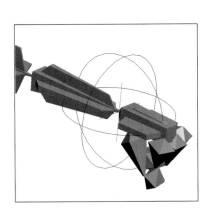

3. First you'll set up the slave tracks for the base thumb bone. Click 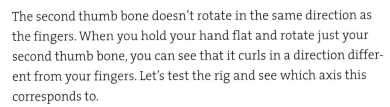 **Add Slave**, and click the base thumb bone. From the pop-up menu, choose *Transform > Rotation > X Rotation*.

4. Repeat the previous step on the same bone two more times, choosing the *Y Rotation* track the first time and *Z Rotation* the second time.

5. Click ✚ **Add Slave**, and click the second thumb bone. From the pop-up menu, choose *Transform > Rotation > X Rotation*.

If your character's second thumb bone rotates on a different axis, use that axis for this step.

6. Turn on **Create Mode**.

7. Set up the following reactions for the thumb:

   - When **CurlThumbL** is -20, stretch the thumb bones to a flat position.

   - When **CurlThumbL** is 100, rotate the thumb bones to a grasping position.

   - When **CurlThumbL** is 200, rotate the thumb bones to a fist position.

▶TIP◀

If you like, you can change the **Curl-IndexFingerL** and **CurlTwoFingersL** values to help you visualize the grasp and fist poses for the thumb. Only the slaves for the **CurlThumbL** master will be affected when you click **Create State**, so changing the other values won't cause any problems in setting up the thumb states.

Test the Reactions

1. Select **CtrlWristL**.

2. Turn on **Auto Key**, and go to frame 10.

3. On the 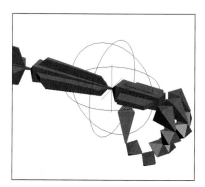 Modify panel, set **CurlTwoFingersL**, **CurlIndexFingerL**, and **CurlThumbL** to -20.

4. Go to frame 20, and change all the custom attributes to 100.

   The fingers should go into the grasping pose.

5. On frame 30, change all the custom attribute values to 200.

   Now the pose should resemble a fist.

6. Turn off **Auto Key**.

7. Scrub the time slider back and forth, and watch the hand as it animates.

8. Save the scene as **CharRig15.max**.

9. To complete the rig, duplicate all these steps on the right hand and save as **CharRig16.max**.

   You'll find a rig with both hands set up on the CD in the file *CharRig16.max*.

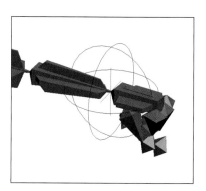

TUTORIAL R12

Completing the Arm Rig

To complete the arm rig, you need a shoulder control.

Rig the Shoulder

The control for the shoulder will work a little differently than the wrist control. It will be the parent object for the entire arm, including the clavicle, but will be positioned not at the base of the clavicle, but between the clavicle and the upper arm. In addition, its pivot point will be aligned with the clavicle's pivot point.

This might seem like a strange construction for the shoulder rig, but once it's set up, you'll see how this helps you control the shoulder.

1. Continue from the previous exercise, or load *CharRig16.max*.

2. Choose *File > Merge* to merge the **Gyro** object from *Control-Shapes.max*.

   You could copy the wrist gyro to make the shoulder gyro, but then the shoulder gyro would have all the wrist's custom attributes on it. By merging it again, you start with a fresh gyro.

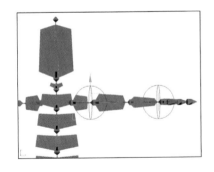

3. Use 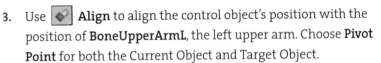 **Align** to align the control object's position with the position of **BoneUpperArmL**, the left upper arm. Choose **Pivot Point** for both the Current Object and Target Object.

   This aligns the control object's position with the upper arm.

4. Name the gyro **CtrlShoulderL**.

   Now you'll move the object's pivot point to match the pivot point of the clavicle bone.

5. On the ⬛ **Hierarchy** panel, click **Affect Pivot Only**.

6. Click ◆ **Align**, then click the left clavicle, **BoneClavicleL**. Align both the position and orientation. Choose **Pivot Point** for the Current Object and Target Object.

7. Turn off **Affect Pivot Only**.

8. 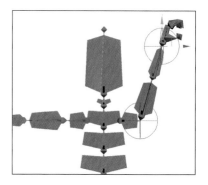 Link **BoneClavicleL** to **CtrlShoulderL**.

9. Link **CtrlShoulderL** to **BoneSpine04**.

Test the Shoulder Rig

1. Turn on **Auto Key**.

2. Go to frame 10.

3. In the Front viewport, move the left wrist control, **CtrlWristL**, upward to extend the arm up, and rotate the wrist control to pose the hand comfortably.

   The shoulder looks stiff and unnatural.

4. In the Front viewport, rotate **CtrlShoulderL** to raise the shoulder.

   This pose looks more natural with the shoulder rotated upward.

   In essence, you're using the control object as a parent for the clavicle. You put the control object between the clavicle and upper arm simply to make it easier to select.

5. Turn off **Auto Key**.

6. Save the scene as **CharRig17.max**.

7. Repeat these steps to set up the shoulder rig for the right arm and save as **CharRig18.max**.

   A scene with both shoulders set up can be found in the file *CharRig18.max* in the *Rigs* folder on the CD.

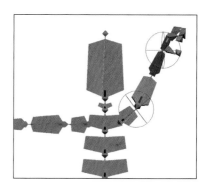

Elbows and Knees

You've got most of the body parts all rigged up: feet, legs, arms, hands, and shoulders. Two of the last parts to rig are the elbows and knees.

You want to be able to make the elbows and knees point in any direction, independently of what the ankles and wrists are doing.

To accomplish this, you'll take advantage of a built-in control for IK chains.

When you experimented with IK chains at the beginning of this chapter, you saw that every IK chain has a swivel angle. You can place a rig control in the scene and use it as a target for the swivel angle. This will enable you to change the swivel angle interactively by moving the target.

Rigging Elbows and Knees

Set up the Knee Control

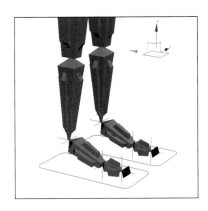

1. Load the file *CharRig18.max* or continue from the previous tutorial.

2. In the Top viewport, create a rectangle about 20 by 20 units in size. Make sure you create a rectangle and not a plane.

3. Name the rectangle **CtrlKneeL**.

4. Move the rectangle so it sits in front of the left knee, a short distance from the leg.

5. Link **CtrlKneeL** to **CtrlFootL**.

   This will keep the knee control near the character no matter where he goes.

6. Select the IK chain at the left foot's ankle.

7. Go to the **Motion** panel.

8. In the IK Solver Properties rollout, click the button under **Pick Target**, and pick **CtrlKneeL**.

   This will cause the joint between the thigh and calf bones to point at **CtrlKneeL** no matter where you move the control.

Test the Knee Control

It will be much easier to see whether the knee rig is working if you bend the knee first.

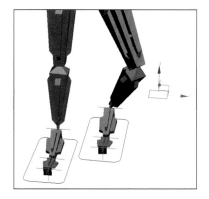

1. Turn on **Auto Key**.

2. Go to frame 10, and move **CtrlFootL** upward to bend the left knee.

3. Move **CtrlKneeL** a short distance in the scene.

    The knee should point to **CtrlKneeL** wherever you move it.

4. Turn off **Auto Key**.

5. Create a control for the right knee, and call it **CtrlKneeR**. Use the same procedure to make it control the right knee.

Set up Elbow Controls

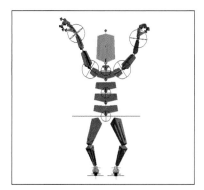

1. Copy one of the knee controls, and place it behind the left elbow.

2. Name the control object **CtrlElbowL**.

3. 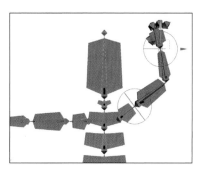 Link **CtrlElbowL** to **CtrlWristL**.

4. Select the IK chain at the left wrist.

5. On the ⊚ **Motion** panel, click the button under **Pick Target**, and pick **CtrlElbowL**.

6. Repeat this procedure for the right elbow.

7. Save the scene as **CharRig19.max**.

Parameter Collector

The Parameter Collector is a floating dialog in which you can place parameters from the scene. It provides one central location for a group of related parameters that might otherwise be found in many different locations in the user interface. For example, you could put all the foot roll and finger curl parameters in one

Parameter Collector dialog. This would allow you to animate the rig's hands and feet without having to select the wrist and foot controls each time.

To open the Parameter Collector, choose *Animation > Parameter Collector*. To add parameters to the dialog, click ⊕ **Add to New Rollout**, and expand the *Objects* listing in the Track View Pick dialog until you find the parameter(s) you want to add to the dialog. You can organize and rename your rollouts with the **Rollouts** options in the dialog.

TUTORIAL R14
Finishing the Rig

To complete the rig, you just need to create an overall control for the legs and another for the body, and tidy things up a little.

Create the Control for the Legs

1. Load the file *CharRig19.max,* or continue from the previous tutorial.

2. In the Top viewport, create a circle shape about twice as wide as the character's body. Name the shape **CtrlLegs**.

3. Align the shape with **BoneSpine01**. In the Align dialog, set both Current Object and Target Object to **Pivot Point**.

4. Link the thigh bones to **CtrlLegs**.

5. Unhide the spine control objects.

6. Link the lowest spine control shape, **CtrlSpineBase**, to **CtrlLegs**.

7. Link the wrist controls to **CtrlLegs**.

    This will cause the arms to move when the spine goes up and down. Some riggers don't like to limit the rig in this way, but I find it easier to work with this arrangement.

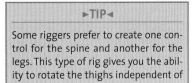

▶TIP◀

Some riggers prefer to create one control for the spine and another for the legs. This type of rig gives you the ability to rotate the thighs independent of the spine.

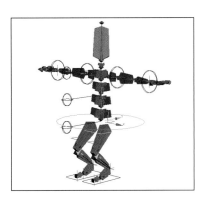

Create an Overall Body Control

You need just one last item: A single object that controls the entire body, so you can easily move the entire character at once. This is essential for placing the character at the start of the animation.

1. In the Top viewport, create a rectangle larger than the **Ctrl-Legs** circle. Name the rectangle **CtrlBody**.

2. Position the rectangle at the bottom of the character's feet.

    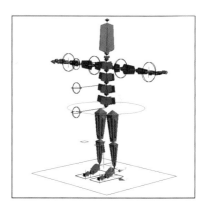

    Now, the only remaining task is to link up the wrist and shoulder controls.

3. 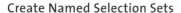 Link **CtrlLegs**, **CtrlFootL**, and **CtrlFootR** to **CtrlBody**.

4. Test the linkage by moving **CtrlBody**.

    When you move **CtrlBody**, the entire hierarchy should go with it.

Create Named Selection Sets

To prepare the rig for animation, you'll create a named selection set for the controls.

1. Select all the control objects (all objects beginning with **Ctrl**).

2. Create a named selection set called **Control Objects**.

3. Select all the IK chains, and create a named selection set called **IK Chains**.

4. On frame 0, remove all existing animation keys from control objects. To do this, select all the control objects, and draw a selection region around the keys on the Trackbar. The keys will turn white when selected. Press **[Delete]** on the keyboard to delete the keys.

5. Save the scene as **CharRig20.max**.

There are more controls you could add to this rig, but these will be sufficient for many types of animation. You'll animate with this rig in the *Animation* section. But before you can do that, you'll need to skin the character with the tools and techniques described in the next chapter.

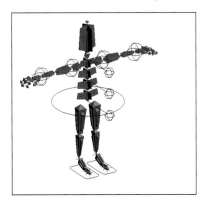

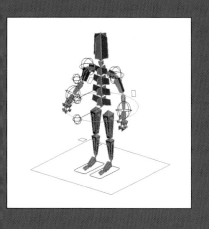

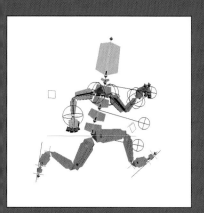

CHAPTER 5

Skinning

The skeleton's in place and rigged for easy movement, but until you attach it to the mesh, it can't move your character. The process of associating the mesh with the bones is known as *skinning*. Technically speaking, skinning is part of the rigging process. However, it requires a set of tools and techniques quite different from those for setting up controls for bones.

The Skin Modifier

In 3ds max, you start the skinning process by applying the Skin modifier to the mesh, and associating bones with the mesh. Each bone influences (deforms) the mesh around it when the bones are animated.

To perform the deformation, each vertex in the mesh receives a specific *weight* from each bone. If the bone completely controls the vertex, the vertex's weight with regard to that bone is 1.0. If the bone has no influence over the vertex, the vertex's weight for that bone is 0.0.

A weight between 0.0 and 1.0 means the vertex is affected by the bone to some degree, but is probably affected by other bones, too. Partial weighting by multiple bones is used at joints such as the elbows, wrists, knees, ankles, hips, and shoulders. At the knee, for example, the vertices are affected by both the thigh and calf bones. A vertex at the top of the knee might have a weight of 0.7 for the thigh bone and 0.3 for the calf. Usually, a vertex's weights for all its bones add up to 1.0.

There are two ways to set vertex weights: With envelopes, and by manual adjustment.

Envelopes

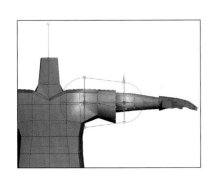

By default, the Skin modifier creates two capsule-shaped areas around each bone called *envelopes*. The vertices that fall within a bone's envelopes are assigned a weight with regard to that bone. You can change the size and shape of envelopes to change the weights of vertices that fall inside it.

Envelopes are useful for roughing out the vertex weights. But with most character rigs, envelopes won't give you enough control over the weights to set up an accurate deformation, particularly at the joints.

Manual Vertex Adjustment

With any character that has arms and legs, you'll need to adjust vertex weights manually. This isn't as scary is it might sound. With a low-polygon mesh such as the one we use in this book, you'll be able to see the results of your manually set weights instantly, and can work intuitively with the weights onscreen.

Manually set vertex weights override any weights assigned by envelopes.

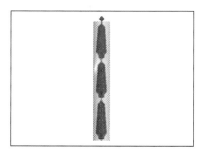

PRACTICE N

Using the Skin Modifier

Here, you'll practice using the Skin modifier on a simple object.

Load the Scene

1. Load the scene *Practice_Skin01.max* from the *Practice* folder on the CD.

    This scene contains a see-through cylinder with three bones. The bones are animated, but the Skin modifier has not been applied to the cylinder.

2. Pull the time slider to see the animation.

    The bones rotate until frame 25.

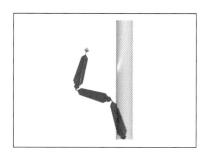

Apply the Skin Modifier

1. Go to frame 0.

    The frame on which you apply the Skin modifier is important. The Skin modifier uses the relationship between the bones and mesh at the current frame to determine the bones' initial influences over vertices.

2. Select the cylinder.

3. Go to the **Modify** panel, and apply the **Skin** modifier to the cylinder.

4. On the Parameters rollout, click **Add**.

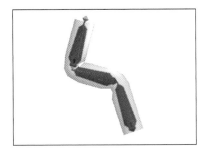

5. In the Select Bones dialog, select all the bones, and click **Select**.

    Now the bones will influence the cylinder.

6. Pull the time slider to see how the mesh responds to the skinning.

    The mesh bends with the bones. However, the mesh looks slightly crumpled at the joints, especially in the topmost joint, where the bending angle is about 90 degrees. This is a typical situation you'll encounter when you skin a character.

Look at the Envelopes

The initial sizes of the envelopes are determined by the sizes of the bones. If the bones are one-half to three-fourths the size of the mesh, the envelopes should encompass the mesh around it.

1. Select the cylinder.

2. Press [**Alt-X**] to make the cylinder look solid.

3. On the **Modify** panel, click **Edit Envelopes**.

    The mesh turns blue, except for one area, which is red. Two capsule-shaped envelopes surround the red area.

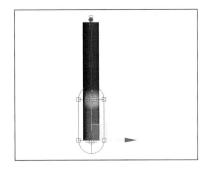

4. In the Parameters rollout, select different bones to see their envelopes.

    Of the pair of envelopes, one is completely inside the other. The one inside is called the *inner envelope,* while the other is the *outer envelope.*

    Ideally, the inner envelope encompasses a non-bending part of the mesh, a place where a rigid bone would be. Outer envelopes are designed to overlap in joint areas, which causes the vertices in those areas to be influenced by both bones to some degree.

Adjust the Envelopes

Each envelope has numerous square-shaped *handles* that define its shape. You can move the handles to change the size and shape of the envelope.

When you're shaping envelopes, the vertices and faces within the envelope change color to tell you whether they're being influenced by the bone, and by how much. Red vertices are completely influenced by the bone, with a weight of 1.0. Vertices and faces gradually change from red to orange to yellow as they are less influenced. Vertices and faces that receive no influence from the envelope, with a weight of 0.0, are blue.

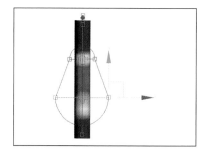

Even though the inner envelopes in this example do not encompass the mesh, the area around them is red. This is because no other bone is influencing that area, so the surrounding outer envelope gives these vertices a weight of 1.0.

1. On any envelope, drag one of the rectangular handles to change the size of the envelope.

    The mesh changes color accordingly, but the shape of the mesh doesn't change.

2. Pull the time slider to frame 25.

3. Select one of the envelopes that influences a joint.

4. Drag one of the handles near the joint to see how the change in the envelope affects the mesh.

    With joints, it's easier to see the influence of envelopes when the joint is bent. This is a very effective way to work. Changing envelopes on any frame affects the skinning throughout the animation.

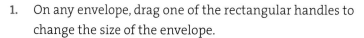

►TIP◄

When changing envelope sizes, make sure **Auto Key** is turned off. Envelope sizes can be animated, but in general, this is not desirable.

Adjust Envelope Directions

The envelope's handles lie on its *cross sections*. These are the circular shapes that set the volume of the envelope at that point. Each envelope also has *directional handles,* two gray handles at each end of the inner envelope. You can move these handles to change the length of the envelope, or the direction in which the envelope lies.

It can be difficult to select directional handles unless you first turn off the ability to select cross-section handles.

1. In the Parameters rollout, uncheck the **Cross Sections** option.

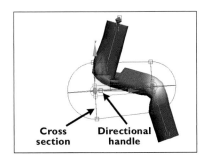

Cross section   Directional handle

2. Select one of the gray handles at the end of an envelope. These are the only handles you are currently allowed to select.

3. Move the handle to change the direction in which the envelope lies.

    Most likely, this change will not improve the way the joints look. This is just to show you how to do this task, as you'll need it when you skin the character.

4. Undo the change to the envelope direction.

5. Check **Cross Sections** to allow selection of the cross-section handles.

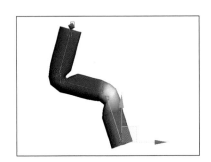

6. Adjust the envelopes at frame 25 until the bends at the joints look as good as you can get them with this method.

    Don't be concerned if the joints look crumpled or messy. You'll fix this in the next set of steps.

7. Save the scene as **Practice_Skin02.max**.

Select Vertices for Manual Adjustment

Now you'll manually adjust the vertex weights to make the cylinder's joints look better when they bend. First, you'll change the display to make it easier to see and select the appropriate vertices.

1. In the Parameters rollout, check **Vertices**.

This will allow you to select vertices for manual adjustment.

2. Right-click the Front viewport label, and choose *Edged Faces* from the drop-down menu.

    This allows you to see the cylinder's vertices more clearly.

3. In the Parameters rollout, uncheck **Envelopes**.

    This will prevent you from accidentally selecting envelopes when you are working with the vertices.

4. In the Display rollout, check **Show No Envelopes**.

    This unclutters the screen so you can work more effectively. You can no longer select a bone by clicking it in a viewport, but you can still select a bone by highlighting its name in the Parameters rollout.

5. In the Parameters rollout, highlight **Bone01**.

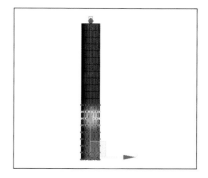

The first part of manual vertex weighting is to figure out which vertices need adjustment, then select them. This can be tricky. It's easiest to see which vertices need adjustment when the mesh is deformed. However, it's easiest to select the vertices when the mesh is not deformed.

To select the appropriate vertices, you'll look at the deformed mesh to locate them, then go back to frame 0 to select them. You'll work with one row of vertices at a time.

6. Pull the time slider to frame 25, and watch the lowest joint closely in the Front viewport. Locate the vertices at the bend that will need adjustment.

7. Keeping your eye on the vertices, move the time slider back to frame 0.

8. Draw a selection region around the highest row of vertices that require adjustment. These vertices are most likely yellow or orange.

    A white box appears around each selected vertex.

> **►TIP◄**
>
> One way to keep track of the vertices that need to be adjusted is to note their colors. Vertices at joints are usually yellow, orange, or pink.

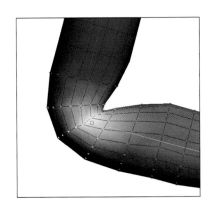

Adjust Vertex Weights

1. Go to frame 25.

2. On the **Modify** panel, locate the **Abs. Effect** parameter in the Weight Properties group.

    This is the parameter that sets the selected vertices' weight for the currently selected bone. The parameter name is short for "absolute effect," which means it sets the vertex weights to exactly the value you enter. If the selected row of vertices have different weights (as they usually do when weights are set by envelopes), the parameter will not show a value at the moment.

3. While watching the Front viewport, use the **Abs. Effect** spinner to increase or decrease this value until the vertices are angled slightly more than the vertices just above them. A value of 0.15 to 0.25 should work well.

4. Go back to frame 0, and select the next lowest row of vertices.

5. Go to frame 25, and change the **Abs. Effect** spinner so the vertices are angled slightly more than the first set.

    When you do this, you're actually setting two sets of weights. The weights for the selected bone are set to the value you set with **Abs. Effect**. The weights for the adjacent bone are adjusted accordingly, so the two sets of weights add up to 1.0. For example, if you set **Abs. Effect** to 0.35, the vertices' weights for the adjacent bone will be automatically adjusted to 0.65.

6. Repeat these steps on one or two more rows of vertices, until the joint looks smooth.

    Now you'll adjust the other joint, which has a more severe bend.

7. In the Parameters rollout, highlight **Bone02**.

8. Use the same method you used before to determine which vertices need to be corrected. Select each row of vertices, and

adjust the **Abs. Effect** parameter for each one until the joint looks as smooth as possible.

With this joint, it's impossible to create a perfectly smooth bend. The angle is so severe that the joint is pinched. This looks unnatural, as the joint loses its original volume at this point. To correct this problem, you'll use another skinning tool, the **Skin Morph** modifier, which is covered later in this chapter.

9. Save the scene as **Practice_Skin03.max**.

Character Skinning

So far, you've learned how to apply the Skin modifier, adjust envelopes, and adjust vertex weights manually. When applying the Skin modifier to a character mesh, there are a few additional considerations.

Choosing Body Parts for Skinning

If two or more mesh parts are going to use the same skeletal structure, you can apply the Skin modifier to all the parts at once. For example, if your character's upper and lower body are separate objects, you can select both objects and apply the Skin modifier to both at the same time. This creates an *instanced modifier* on the modifier stack, where changing Skin parameters for one object would change them for all objects to which Skin was applied.

For the character in this book, you'll apply the Skin modifier to the body only. You could apply it to the head and hair too, but this isn't necessary since the head and hair won't need to deform with the bones; most likely, you'll want the head to nod, shake, and tilt, but not deform. Instead, you'll link the head mesh to the head bone, and animate the head by rotating the neck control.

> ►TIP◄
>
> When working on your own characters, you might encounter situations where it's appropriate to apply the Skin modifier to the head. For example, you would do this if you wanted to animate the head of a rubbery character bending or deforming.

TurboSmooth and Skinning

You'll most likely want to apply the TurboSmooth modifier to a low-polygon character to smooth it out before rendering. However, you should put the Skin modifier *below* TurboSmooth on the stack. This minimizes the number of vertices you'll have to adjust with the Skin modifier. You can apply the Skin modifier below TurboSmooth by highlighting the Editable Mesh (or Editable Poly) listing, then applying the Skin modifier.

When the modifiers are arranged in this way, the model still deforms correctly, and the result is beautifully smoothed. If you put the Skin modifier *above* TurboSmooth, the result will not be any better than if you put the Skin modifier below TurboSmooth, and you will only make more work for yourself.

In this book, to simplify things, you'll apply the Skin modifier to a model that has no TurboSmooth modifier on it. After the skinning process is complete, you'll apply the TurboSmooth modifier to the mesh and see the result.

Skin Pose

The Skin modifier relies on the placement of the bones in relationship to the mesh to make its associations correctly. Right now, the bones are placed correctly, but soon you'll be animating the rig.

Setting the *skin pose* allows you to return to the pose used for skinning at any time during the animation process. The skin pose saves the positions of bones, IK chains, and any control objects.

You can set the skin pose by choosing *Character > Set Skin Pose*. Later, if you want to make objects return to the skin pose, you can select the objects and choose *Character > Assume Skin Pose*.

Setting the Skin Pose

Check the Rig

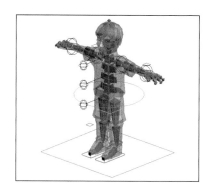

1. Load the file *CharRig20.max* from your *Rigs* folder, or from the *Rigs* folder on the CD.

2. Unhide all parts of the mesh.

3. If the character mesh isn't see-through, select all mesh parts and press **[Alt-X]** to make it so.

4. Make sure you're at frame 0.

5. Check the model carefully to make sure the bones go through the appropriate parts of the mesh.

   For the hands, feet, and head, you want the mesh to reach the start of the nub at the end of the bone chain. The mesh should not extend beyond the start of the nub.

> ►TIP◄
>
> You can unhide the mesh by choosing the *Mesh* selection set, and answering **Yes** on the window that appears. This also selects all the mesh parts for the next step.

6. If necessary, put the bones in their correct locations by using the rig controls, or by moving or rotating the bones themselves. This step might take a while to complete, but you'll find it's time well spent when you skin the character.

   The bones for the fingers and feet are the most likely to be out of place. For the finger bones, you can rotate a bone on any axis for which it does not have a reaction set up in the Reaction Manager.

   If necessary, you can modify the mesh at the **Vertex** sub-object level to fit the bones. If you change one side of the body, you can use the **Symmetry** modifier to mirror the change to the other side of the body. If you use the Symmetry modifier, collapse the mesh to an Editable Mesh afterward.

> ►TIP◄
>
> To adjust the finger bones, select **Ctrl-WristL** and change the custom attributes to make the fingers curl a little to match the mesh. If they won't fit exactly, adjust the mesh itself. If you have to adjust the mesh, change the User or Perspective viewport display to *Smooth + Highlights* and *Edged Faces*.

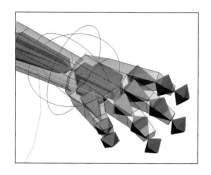

Set the Skin Pose

1. Make sure you are at frame 0.

2. Select all the objects in the scene, including the bones, IK chains, control objects, and character mesh.

3. Choose *Character > Set Skin Pose*. When you're asked if you really want to set the skin pose, answer **Yes**.

4. Create a *Skinning* folder on your hard disk.

5. Save the scene in the *Skinning* folder as **CharSkin01.max**.

► TIP ◄

Instead of changing the mesh, you might find it more convenient to stretch or shorten bones. To do this, you can select the bone you want to stretch or shorten, choose *Character > Bone Tools* (make sure **Freeze Length** is turned off), move its child bone to change its length, then select the stretched or lengthened bone and turn on **Freeze Length**.

Test Animation

Part of the skinning process is setting up a simple test animation. The test animation should put the character through the most extreme poses it's likely to make during the final animation. These poses will enable you to test the accuracy of the skinning and fine-tune it for the best deformation.

You can think of the test animation as a short exercise program for the character. As the character stretches and bends in a variety of ways, you'll be able to check that the skin responds properly in these poses.

A test animation should include bending the knees and elbows, clenching the fists, bending over, and any other actions the character might do over the course of the animation.

► TIP ◄

In your test animation, avoid putting the character in unnatural poses that are not likely to be used, such as swinging his leg over his shoulder (unless the character is a contortionist). Adjusting the skinning for unnatural poses is difficult, time-consuming, and unnecessary.

For at least half the poses in your test animation, position the two sides of the character symmetrically. For example, if you raise both hands in the air, try to make the left arm mirror the right. Posing the character symmetrically will enable you to use skin morphing more effectively.

Setting up the Test Animation

To help with the skinning process, you'll set up a short test animation with extreme poses. This will help you spot trouble areas and make adjustments after the Skin modifier is applied.

Prepare for Animation

You need to see only the bones and control objects to set up the test animation.

1. Load the file *CharSkin01.max* from your *Skinning* folder or the CD.

2. Hide the body, head, and hair.

3. Freeze the bones.

   You'll animate the character using the control objects only. Freezing the bones will prevent you from accidentally selecting them.

4. Select all the control objects, and delete any animation keys for them.

5. You'll need a few more frames to create the complete test animation. Click ⏹ **Time Configuration**. In the Time Configuration dialog, change **Length** to 120. Click **OK** to set the new animation length.

>**►TIP◄**
>
>You can quickly freeze the bones by selecting them with the **Bones** selection set you created earlier, then right-clicking and choosing *Freeze Selection* from the Quad menu.

Animate the Arms and Knees

1. Turn on **Auto Key**.

2. Go to frame 10. In the Top viewport, move the wrist controls toward the front of the character until the wrist controls just touch the shoulder controls. Rotate the wrist controls so the hands face forward.

   This creates a symmetrical animation with the elbows bent.

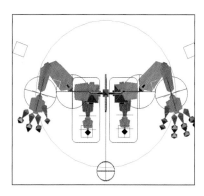

Rotate the wrist controls in the Local coordinate system. This way, the rotation gizmo will match the wrist control's rotation, and it will be easier to see what you're doing.

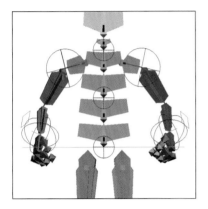

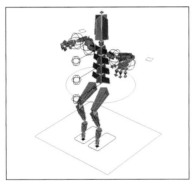

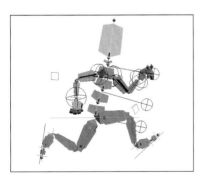

3. On frame 20, move the wrist controls so the character's hands are by its sides. Rotate the wrist controls as necessary to pose the hands naturally, and rotate the clavicles downward slightly. You can also curl the fingers using the custom attributes on the wrist control.

   This gives you three poses for the arms: Straight out at the sides at frame 0, bent at frame 10, and by the sides at frame 20.

4. You can also set a few poses for the feet to help you see how they deform as they roll off the ground. On frame 10, move the left forward and the right foot back.

5. On frame 10, animate each foot's **Roll** parameter to 90.

6. On frame 20, set each **Roll** parameter back to 0.

7. Scrub the time slider to see the animation.

Set Run Poses

By putting the character into a running pose, you'll be able to test the skinning at the hips, knees, shoulders, and elbows.

1. Go to frame 20. Select both foot controls, and right-click the time slider. In the Create Key dialog, click **OK**. This sets a key at frame 20 to keep the feet from moving until this frame.

2. Go to frame 30, and pose the body in a runner's position with the right leg and left arm in front, as shown. Rotate and move the foot, hand, and clavicle controls, and move **CtrlKnee** and **CtrlElbow** as needed to make the pose as natural as possible.

   Rotate the spine controls to make the character lean forward. You can also rotate the clavicles slightly to bend in the directions of the arms.

3. Go to frame 40 and reverse the pose, putting the left leg in front and the right arm in back. Reverse the arm and clavicle positions as well.

You'll need to pose the character manually to reverse the pose. There is no automatic way to mirror a pose.

4. The legs and arms are cramped at frame 35 as they pass between the runner's poses. You can straighten out the legs by copying the foot control keys from frame 0 to 35. First, select both foot controls.

5. Go to frame 35.

6. Right-click the time slider. In the Create Key dialog, set **Source** to 0. Make sure **Position** and **Rotation** are turned on, and click **OK**.

    This copies all the foot control keys from frame 0 to 35.

7. On frame 35, move the wrist controls down to uncramp the arms. Rotate the wrist controls as you like.

8. Save the scene as **CharSkin02.max**.

Create Spine and Leg Animations

The only parts of the body that you haven't really animated yet are the neck and spine.

1. Select all the control objects. On frame 50, choose *Character > Assume Skin Pose*.

    This will put all selected objects back in the skin pose. If **Auto Key** is on, keys are set for the selected objects at the current frame.

2. On frame 50, bend the spine backward to make the character arch his back. Rotate the clavicles back a little, and position the arms slightly behind the body.

3. On frame 60, bend the spine forward. Rotate the clavicles forward, and move the arms slightly in front of the body.

4. Select all the control objects. On frame 70, choose *Character > Assume Skin Pose*.

5. On frame 70, raise the character's arms over his head, as if reaching for something on a high shelf. Be sure to rotate the clavicles upward to suit the arm pose.

►TIP◄

The character's body has some bulk to it, so keep the arms a short distance away from the body. Rotate the foot, hand, and clavicle controls before working with the knee and elbow controls. Rotating the foot, hand, and clavicle controls to the correct orientations will usually put the knee and elbow controls in the right place to make the knees and elbows bend correctly.

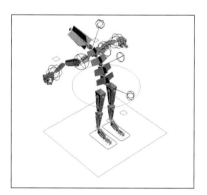

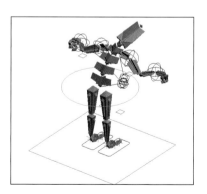

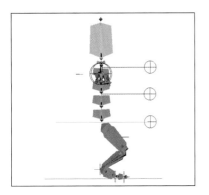

6. On frame 70, rotate the neck control to make the character turn his head to one side.

7. On frame 80, rotate the neck control to turn the character's head to the other side.

8. On frame 90, choose *Character > Assume Skin Pose* to put the character back in its original pose.

You'll also need some symmetrical knee bends, as opposed to the asymmetrical bends you made with the runner's pose. The symmetrical knee bends will come in handy when you use skin morphs later in this chapter.

9. On frame 100, move **CtrlLegs** down to make the knees bend by approximately 90 degrees.

   This is about the maximum angle you'll need the knees to bend during the animation process.

Move the Entire Body

You need one last key to move the entire body control. This will enable you to test that all mesh vertices are being deformed by the Skin modifier.

1. On frame 110, select all the control objects, and choose *Character > Assume Skin Pose*.

2. On frame 120, move the body control to the left or right by a short distance to move the entire rig.

Check the Animation

Our test animation is now complete.

1. Scrub the time slider to see the animation.

   This is an unusual animated sequence. We've made no attempt to balance the character's weight or make the transitions realistic. This animation's sole purpose is to enable us to assist with the skinning process.

If you like, you can make adjustments to the animation to make the transitions between poses smoother, but it's not necessary.

2. Turn off **Auto Key**.

3. Save the scene as **CharSkin03.max**.

    If you have trouble creating this animation, load the file *CharSkin03.max* from the *Skinning* folder on the CD, and look at the animation in the file.

TUTORIAL S3

Skinning the Character

Now you're ready to apply the Skin modifier to the character and adjust its skinning. But first, a little preparation is in order.

Prepare the Mesh for Skinning

1. Load the file *CharSkin03.max,* or continue from the last tutorial.

2. Unfreeze the bones.

3. Unhide the character body, head, and hair.

    You'll link the hair and head to the head bone to make them move with the mesh.

4. [icon] Link the hair mesh to the head mesh.

5. [icon] Link the head mesh to **BoneHead**.

6. Select the character's body mesh. The head and hair should not be selected.

If the **TurboSmooth** modifier has been applied to the body mesh, you'll need to remove it before applying the **Skin** modifier, or apply the Skin modifier below TurboSmooth. Here, we'll remove it and put it back later.

7. If you've applied the **TurboSmooth** modifier to the body mesh, remove it by highlighting it in the modifier stack and clicking [icon] **Remove modifier from the stack**.

> **▶TIP◀**
>
> To link the head mesh to **BoneHead,** you can select the head mesh, click **Select and Link,** then click **Select by Name** on the main toolbar. In the Select Parent dialog, choose **BoneHead**.

Apply the Skin Modifier

1. Go to frame o.

    The character is in its skin pose at this frame, so this is a good frame at which to apply the **Skin** modifier.

2. Apply the **Skin** modifier to the mesh.

3. In the Parameters rollout, click **Add**. Select all the bones. You can do this easily by typing in the prefix **Bone** at the top of the dialog to select all objects with that prefix. Do not select IK chains, control objects, or any other objects in the scene.

4. Scrub the time slider to see the test animation.

    If the mesh moves along with the bones in a general way, then you've associated the bones and mesh correctly. Most likely, some parts of the mesh won't move with the bones. You'll fix this in the steps that follow.

When you assigned the bones to the **Skin** modifier, you also included the nub bones. These bones are unnecessary for skinning, and could cause problems if their envelopes extend into the mesh.

5. In the Parameters rollout, highlight each bone that ends in **NubL** or **NubR**, and click the **Remove** button at the top of the rollout after highlighting each one.

    This removes the nubs from the skinning process, and saves you extra work.

6. Save the scene as **CharSkin04.max**.

Look at the Envelopes

Next, you'll start adjusting the skin settings to make the mesh deform more accurately.

►TIP◄

You might find it helpful to work in *Smooth + Highlights* mode with *Edged Faces* turned on so you can see the vertex colors.

1. Hide everything in the scene except the body mesh.

    You don't need the bones and control objects to be visible while you're adjusting envelopes. The same goes for the head and hair.

2. Turn off see-through mode for the mesh by pressing **[Alt-X]**.

3. Go to frame 0.

4. Select the body mesh. In the Parameters rollout, click **Edit Envelopes**.

5. Click on various envelopes on the character to see what they look like.

▸TIP◂

You can also access envelope-editing mode by expanding the *Skin* modifier on the stack and highlighting the *Envelope* sub-object.

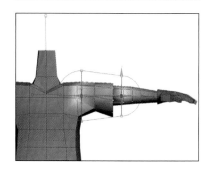

Perform Rough Adjustments on Envelopes

Now you can start adjusting the envelopes for the mesh.

Don't spend a lot of time puzzling over the envelopes at this point. The idea here is to quickly adjust them so they're roughly the right size for the mesh. You should spend no more than two or three minutes on each envelope.

1. Start your adjustments with the legs. Click the left thigh envelope, and adjust it so it encompasses the left thigh but not the right.

   You can select the envelope by clicking it in a viewport, or by selecting **BoneThighL** from the Parameters rollout. You can also change a cross section's size by moving a handle on the cross section in a viewport, or by changing the **Radius** parameter in the Envelope Properties group. This option is available only if you've selected a cross-section handle.

2. When you think you've done a decent job of adjusting the thigh envelope, click the ⬚ **Copy** button in the Envelope Properties group.

3. Select the right thigh envelope, and click ⬚ **Paste**.

   This pastes the copied envelope to the right thigh.

4. Next, click the left calf. Work with this envelope for a few minutes, then copy and paste it to the other side.

5. Continue on with the feet, arms, head, and spine, copying and pasting envelopes when you can.

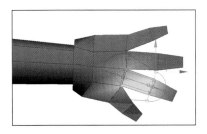

►TIP◄

Recall that the head part of the body mesh is really just a nub sticking out of the character's neck. The head envelope only needs to encompass this nub, not the head or hair meshes.

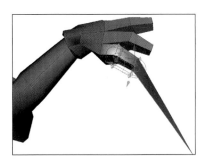

6. In the Top viewport, zoom in on the fingers, and adjust their envelopes. Make sure that each finger envelope affects only the vertices for that finger joint.

   If an envelope looks OK to you, or if you're not sure, leave it and go on to the next one. You're looking only for envelopes that obviously need adjustment.

7. Check the envelopes for the palms and head. These envelopes are often too large, and will need to be made smaller so they encompass the appropriate vertices.

Correct the Finger Envelopes

Note: The problems described in the rest of this section might not exactly match the problems you have with your own skinned character. But chances are they'll apply to some part of your character, and you can use these solutions for any part of the character, as needed.

Now you can use the test animation to help you spot problems with the skinning. A common problem is the hand and finger envelopes not being large enough, so some vertices aren't assigned to any bone. You'll use the animation to spot and fix this problem if it has occurred with your mesh.

1. Scrub between frames 0 and 10.

2. Look for any parts of the hand or fingers that are left behind by the animation, and see if you can figure out which bone the vertices should belong to. Rotate the view to get a good look, and scrub to earlier frames if necessary to see where the mesh is pulling out.

   In the picture shown, the vertices that stayed behind belong to the last pinky link.

3. Move to a frame where you can clearly see vertices that have stayed behind.

4. In a viewport or in the Parameters rollout, select the bone that the wayward vertices should belong to.

5. Move one of the envelope handles away from the bone until the mesh snaps into place.

   You can also use the **Radius** parameter in the Envelope Properties group to increase the size of the cross section and make the vertices snap into place.

   If a small change to the cross section didn't fix the problem, then you've probably selected the wrong envelope or cross section. Undo your work and try again with a different cross section or envelope.

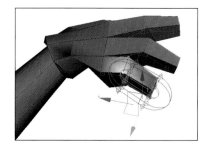

6. Copy and paste the envelope to the other side of the body. If there's a similar problem on the other side of the body, this will often solve it.

7. Look for other areas on the hands where the mesh doesn't follow the bones, and use the same procedure to fix the envelopes.

   Don't work on other parts of the body just yet. The goal now is simply to have all parts of the hands follow the appropriate bones.

8. Save your work as **CharSkin05.max**.

TUTORIAL S4

Weighting Vertices Manually

If you scrub the time slider to frame 10, you can see that the shorts and shirt don't follow along with the animation correctly. You'll fix this by adjusting vertices manually.

Because the right and left pants legs are so close together, it's impossible to weight them correctly with envelopes. For example, if you make the right thigh envelope large enough to encompass all the right thigh vertices, the envelope also encompasses part of the left thigh.

Even if you had modeled the pants legs farther apart, you would still have difficulty getting the correct weighting with envelopes alone. Manual weighting is the only way to get professional results with rigging.

Weight the Pants

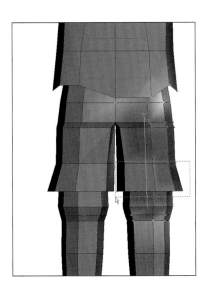

1. Continue with the scene from the previous tutorial, or load *CharSkin05.max* from the *Skinning* folder on the CD. If you load the file from the CD, select the body mesh and turn on **Edit Envelopes** on the **Modify** panel.

2. In the Select group, check the **Vertices** checkbox, and uncheck **Cross Sections** and **Envelopes**.

   This will enable you to select individual vertices on the pants legs.

3. In the Display rollout, check **Show No Envelopes**.

   This will make it easier to see the selected vertices.

4. In the Front viewport, zoom in on the thighs.

5. In the Parameters rollout, select **BoneThighL**.

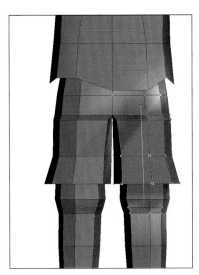

6. On frame 0, draw a selection region around the vertices that make up the lower part of the shorts on the left leg. Each vertex is surrounded by a white box to indicate that it's selected.

7. In the Weight Properties group, change the **Abs. Effect** parameter to 1.0.

   This assigns all the selected vertices to the left thigh bone. The mesh in that area turns red to indicate it receives all its influence from this bone.

8. Select **BoneThighR**, and select the vertices at the bottom of the right pants leg. Change **Abs. Effect** to 1.0.

If you scrub the time slider, you'll see that the bottoms of the pants legs now follow their respective thigh bones.

9. Save the scene as **CharSkin06.max**.

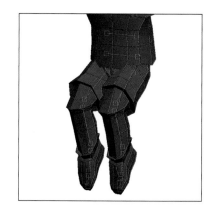

Weight the Sleeves

You can use the same technique to make the shirt sleeves follow the arms.

1. On frame 0, zoom in to the left arm in the Front viewport.

2. In the Parameters rollout, select **BoneUpperArmL**.

3. Draw a selection region around the two rows of vertices at the end of the sleeves to select them, and change **Abs. Effect** to 1.0.

4. Pull the time slider to see the effect on the sleeves.

   The end of the sleeve moves with the arm as it should, but the sleeve passes through the body on some frames, and the vertices near the shoulder twist too much. You'll fix these problems later.

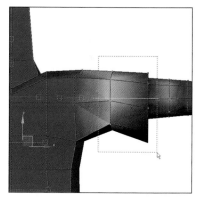

5. Perform the same procedure on the right arm, selecting **BoneUpperArmR** and setting its end-of-sleeve vertices to an **Abs. Effect** value of 1.0.

6. Save the scene as **CharSkin07.max**.

Look for Wayward Vertices

Now you can use the animation to help you find vertices that need correction. The first step is to find vertices that have no weighting at all, so you can make them follow the body.

1. Unhide the body mesh, and hide the bones and control objects.

2. Pull the time slider between frames 110 and 120.

   If any vertices stay behind when **CtrlBody** moves to the side, this means the vertices aren't assigned to any bone at all. You'll weight these manually.

Fix Wayward Vertices

1. Select the body mesh, and turn on **Edit Envelopes**.

2. Pull the time slider back and forth to identify a vertex or group of vertices that are not moving with the body.

3. On any frame, select a vertex or group of vertices that should all move with the same bone.

4. In the Parameters rollout, highlight the bone that the vertices should move with.

   If you're not sure which bone to select, take a guess. You can always change the vertex weights later.

5. Pull the time slider to frame 120.

6. Set **Abs. Effect** to 1.0.

   The vertices will snap to the mesh.

7. Repeat this process for every wayward vertex.

   This ensures that every vertex on the body is assigned to at least one bone, and you won't be distracted by wayward vertices as you weight the rest of the body.

8. Save the scene as **CharSkin08.max**.

Weight the Left Foot

So far, you've used manual weighting to make specific vertices follow one bone only. Now it's time to start weighting the vertices that follow two or three different bones.

This is where the real work begins. The first time you perform these tasks, you might find that you make a mess of things. If that happens, just go to frame 0, select the vertices that are giving you trouble, and weight them back to 1.0 on one bone or another.

1. Go to frame 0.

2. In the Left viewport, zoom in on the feet.

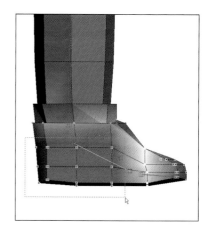

We'll start with the feet and ankles, since these vertices need to be weighted on two bones only. Your first task is to set up some working weights that will provide a good foundation for the rest of the foot weighting.

3. Select the vertices at the heel and middle part of the foot.

4. In the Front viewport, deselect the vertices on the right foot. You'll work with only the left foot for now, and mirror the settings to the other side of the body later on.

5. Select **BoneFootL**, and change **Abs. Effect** to 1.0.

    For starters, the heel should be weighted completely to the foot bone, and the tips of the toes should be weighted to the toe bone. The area at the ball of the foot where it bends should be weighted halfway between the two.

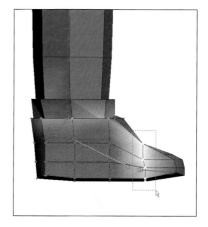

6. Select the vertices at the ball of the foot, and set **Abs. Effect** to 0.5.

7. Select **BoneToeL**, and set **Abs. Effect** to 0.5.

8. Select the vertices at the toe, and set **Abs. Effect** to 1.0.

    This gives you a starting point for weighting the vertices at the ball of the foot.

Adjust the Foot Weights

1. Pull the time slider to frame 5.

    As you watch the animation, ignore the way the ankle or other parts of the body react. You should concern yourself only with the ball of the foot for now. If the ball of the foot

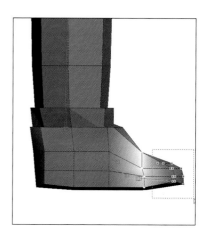

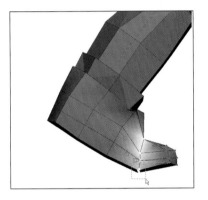

slides when the heel comes up, then the vertices at the bottom of the ball will need to be fully weighted to the toe.

2. Select the vertices at the bottom of the ball of the foot.

3. In the Front viewport, deselect the vertices in the right foot.

4. Make sure **BoneToeL** is selected, and set **Abs. Effect** to 1.0.

Adjust the Ankle

Next, you'll need to use your judgment to adjust the ankle weights. Let's set up some weights for the foot and calf as a starting point.

1. Go to frame 40, where the left foot is raised for the running pose.

2. Select all the vertices at the left ankle.

3. For both **BoneCalfL** and **BoneFootL**, set **Abs. Effect** to 0.5.

    The ankle will snap to a more realistic bend, but it still needs some work. To fix the bend, you'll work with one row of vertices at a time.

4. Select the topmost row of vertices in the ankle.

5. While watching the viewport, use the **Abs. Effect** spinner to gradually increase or decrease this value until the selected vertices follow the calf bone more than the foot bone.

    It doesn't matter whether you have **BoneCalfL** or **BoneFootL** currently selected. Changing the **Abs. Effect** for one of these bones will automatically change it for the other. For example, if you increase the **Abs. Effect** value for **BoneCalfL** to 0.6, it will automatically reduce for **BoneFootL** to 0.4. The selected vertices' weights for both bones will always add up to 1.0.

6. Select the next row of vertices on the ankle. Adjust the **Abs. Effect** value as necessary.

If your character has more rows of vertices at the ankle, continue doing this for each row of vertices until the ankle bend looks as natural as possible.

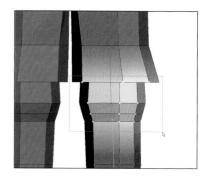

7. Save the scene as **CharSkin09.max**.

Weight the Left Knee

You'll use the same process to weight the left knee's vertices.

1. Go to frame 0.

2. In the Front viewport, select all the vertices at the left knee, including the last row of vertices on the pant leg.

3. For **BoneCalfL** and **BoneThighL**, set **Abs. Effect** to 0.5.

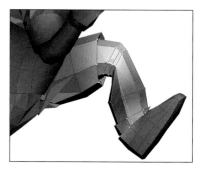

4. Select the topmost row of vertices on the knee (the lowest vertices on the pant leg).

5. Go to frame 40, where the knee is at its maximum bend.

6. Adjust the **Abs. Effect** value until the knee looks better.

7. Do the same for each row of vertices, selecting them on frame 0 and adjusting **Abs. Effect** on frame 40 so for **BoneCalfL** and **BoneThighL** you can see how the knee responds.

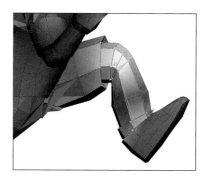

8. Check the skinning on frame 30, where the left knee is behind the body.

   Using this technique, you'll be able to make a big improvement to the way mesh deforms, but the knee will still lose some of its volume as it bends. In addition, the shorts might pass through the leg on frame 30. You can fix these problems later with skin morphing.

9. Save the scene as **CharSkin10.max**.

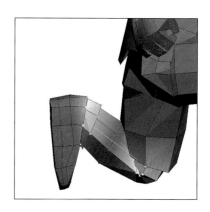

Skin Mirror

The Skin modifier's Mirror Mode allows you to paste envelope settings and vertex weights from one side of the character's body to the other. To use this tool, you must first access the Skin Modifier's **Envelope** sub-object level. Then you can turn on **Mirror Mode** on the Mirror Parameters rollout.

To mirror the settings, select vertices on the mesh for which envelopes and vertex weights have already been set up. The Skin modifier uses a mirror plane, which defaults to the location and orientation of the mesh's pivot point.

The Skin modifier uses a *threshold,* or distance from the mirror plane, to determine the mirrored targets. The threshold is set by the Mirror Thresh value. You increase the **Mirror Thresh** value until the selected vertices turn yellow, and the corresponding vertices on the opposite side of the body turn green (on the right side) or blue (on the left side).

When the vertices are the appropriate colors, click **Mirror Paste** to paste all envelope and vertex settings from the yellow side to the opposite side.

TUTORIAL S5

Mirroring Skin Weights

1. Continue with the file you created in the last tutorial, or load the file *CharSkin10.max* from the *Skinning* folder on the CD.

2. Select the body mesh.

3. Select the *Skin* modifier on the stack, and go to the **Envelope** sub-object level.

4. In the Parameters rollout, under the Select group, make sure **Vertices** is checked.

5. In the Mirror Parameters rollout, click **Mirror Mode** to turn it on.

The panel on the left reads:

- Mirror Parameters
- Mirror Mode
- Mirror Paste
- Paste Green to Blue Bones
- Paste Blue to Green Bones
- Paste Green to Blue Verts
- Paste Blue to Green Verts
- Mirror Plane: X
- Mirror Offset: 0.0
- Mirror Thresh.: 3.681
- Display Projection
- Default Display
- Manual Update
- Update

6. In the Front viewport, select all the vertices on the character's left side. This is the side of the character that's on your right when viewed in the Front viewport. Do not select the vertices down the center of the character.

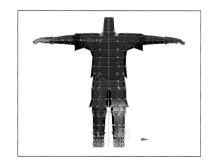

Some of the vertices on the left side turn yellow to indicate they are selected, while some of the vertices on the right turn green. Many are still red, indicating they will not be affected by the mirroring operation in their current state.

7. Increase the **Mirror Thresh** value and watch the character in the Front viewport. Vertices on the character's left side will turn from red to yellow as you change this value, while vertices on its right will change from red to green.

When the vertices stop changing colors, this means you've increased the **Mirror Thresh** value enough to include all the vertices in the mesh.

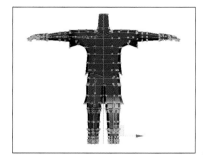

8. Click **Mirror Paste**.

This pastes the envelope and vertex settings from the selected side (left) to the opposite side (right).

9. Turn off **Mirror Mode** and test the changes by pulling the time slider to see how the right foot reacts to the animation.

If the right foot doesn't deform correctly, the most likely cause is that you didn't increase the **Mirror Thresh** value high enough before pasting. Select the left side vertices and try again.

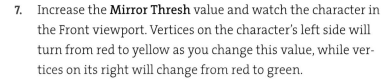
►TIP◄
You can also use Mirror Mode on just a small selection of vertices, such as an arm or hand.

10. Save the scene as **CharSkin11.max**.

Weighting on Multiple Bones

The hips and shoulders are the most difficult parts of a character to skin correctly. Each part of the hip is affected by both the spine and at least one thigh bone. Some vertices, such as those at the center of the hips, are affected by both thigh bones as well as the spine. You also have the added challenge here of a T-shirt that hangs below the waist.

You might be tempted to weight one side and use Mirror Mode to pass the settings to the other side. But because most parts of the hips are affected by both thigh bones, this isn't a very useful solution.

Instead, you'll adjust the skinning at the hips with plain old vertex weighting. One tool you can use to apply multiple weights to bones is the Weight Table. You can access the Weight Table by clicking the **Weight Table** button on the Skin modifier's Parameters rollout.

This table displays vertex weights, with bones across the top and vertices down the left side. You can also change weights directly on the table. This is useful for weighting vertices that are affected by more than two bones, such as the vertices at the buttocks.

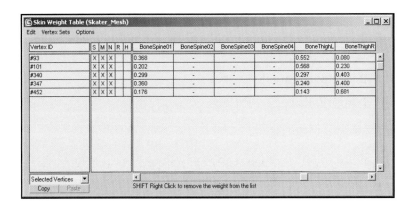

TUTORIAL 56

Weighting on Multiple Bones

The two areas that will benefit most from multiple bone weighting are the hips and shoulders. You'll begin working on these areas by setting some basic weights as a starting point.

Set Initial Shoulder Weights

1. Continue with the file you created in the previous tutorial, or load the file *CharRig11.max* from the *Rigs* folder on the CD.

2. Select the body mesh, go to the **Modify** panel, and turn on **Edit Envelopes** for the **Skin** modifier.

3. Go to frame 0.

   The vertices at the shoulders are influenced by the topmost spine bone (BoneSpine04), the clavicle bone, and the upper arm bone.

4. In the Front viewport, select the vertical set of vertices that make up the shirt's armhole seam.

5. In the Parameters rollout, select **BoneClavicleL**, and set **Abs. Effect** to 0.5.

6. For the same set of vertices, select **BoneSpine04** and **Bone-UpperArmL**, and set **Abs. Effect** to 0.25 for each one.

7. Select the next set of vertices between the armhole and the sleeve edge. Set **Abs. Effect** values as follows:

BoneClavicleL	0.5
BoneUpperArmL	0.5
BoneSpine04	0

Set Initial Hip Weights

1. In the Front viewport, select the vertices at the hips, including the vertices at the creases of the thighs.

2. In the Parameters rollout, select **BoneSpine01**, and set **Abs. Effect** to 1.0.

3. Select **BoneThighL**.

4. Working your way down the character's left side, select three or four rows of vertices at a time, and set weights as follows:

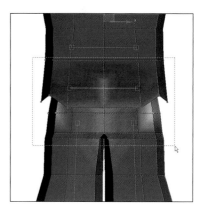

Near the waist:	0.1
Shirttail:	0.2
Hip below shirttail:	0.6
Crease at thighs:	0.8
Center crotch area:	0.4

When you change a value, the value of the weight for **Bone-Spine01** will automatically be reduced to make the total weight 1.0.

Mirror Initial Weights

1. Using **Mirror Mode**, mirror the weights from the left side of the body to the right. Be sure to include the shoulders when you mirror the weights.

   The center crotch vertex weights will not mirror to the other side as they're at the exact center of the body.

2. Select the center crotch vertices, and weight them to 0.4 for **BoneThighR**.

3. Save the scene as **CharSkin12.max**.

Fine-Tune the Hip Weights

Now you can start fine-tuning the weights. This process must be done on just one or two vertices at a time. You'll start the process on a frame where the thighs don't bend much.

1. Pull the time slider to a frame where the thighs just begin to bend, such as frame 23 or 24.

2. Use ⟨ ⟩ **Arc Rotate** to look at the hips from all angles.

3. When you see a vertex that isn't deforming correctly, select the appropriate thigh bone, select the vertex, and use the **Abs. Effect** spinner to increase or decrease the bone's influence over the vertex.

   The crease at the thighs is there for a reason: To allow the pants legs to crease when the leg bends forward. Be sure to allow the crease to occur at that spot when you adjust vertex weights.

4. When you've finished adjusting vertices on a particular frame, move to the next frame to see how the leg looks. Adjust vertex weights as needed.

▶TIP◀

In addition to adjusting the vertex weights on each individual thigh, you'll find that the hips deform more smoothly if you make each thigh affect the vertices in the opposite thigh's crease by a very small amount, such as 0.1 or less.

5. When you think you've done a decent job of weighting, check the weights at frames 30 and 40, where the bend is most extreme.

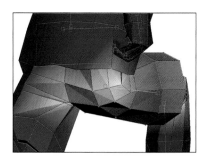

Take care not to let the buttock area lose its shape when the legs bend at their most extreme poses. You can help the buttocks keep their shape by increasing the **Abs. Effect** of **Bone-Spine01** for these vertices.

Don't be concerned if the pants go through the shirt at extreme poses. When the leg is posed like this in the final animation, the pants will hide the shirt from view.

6. Rotate around in the User viewport, and adjust the thigh and hip vertices at various frames until it looks as good as you can get it.

If something strange is happening with the vertices and you can't figure out what it is, it's possible the vertices are being influenced by another bone that you don't know about. To find out which bones are influencing a vertex or set of vertices, you can use the Weight Table.

►TIP◄

Professional riggers sometimes spend several days adjusting vertex weights, so don't be surprised if your first try takes a few hours.

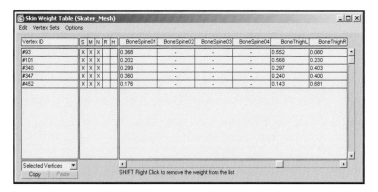

7. In the Weight Properties group, click **Weight Table**. At the lower left of the Weight Table window, choose *Selected Vertices* from the drop-down menu.

You can scroll the display to the left or right to see which bones affect the selected vertices. The weight for each bone that affects the vertices is listed under that bone on the chart.

8. If a vertex is being affected by a bone that shouldn't influence it, you can change its weight right on the chart. Either type a new value into the chart or drag on a value to change it. Dragging to the left lowers a value, while dragging to the right increases it.

   As you change one vertex weight, the vertex's other weights will also increase or decrease proportionally to keep the total weight to 1.0.

9. When you're satisfied with the hip weights, save the scene as **CharSkin13.max**.

10. You can use the same process to fine-tune the shoulder weights. Select one or two vertices at a time, and adjust the **Abs. Effect** value for the clavicle and upper arm on that side of the body. When you've finished with the shoulder, you can mirror the weights to the other side by selecting just the vertices at the shoulder and using **Mirror Paste**.

    It might be difficult to make the shoulders work exactly as you'd like. If this is the case, do the best you can for now. Later, you'll learn how to use skin morphing to solve weighting problems at joints.

11. After you have adjusted the shoulder weights, save the scene as **CharSkin14.max**.

Check the Mesh with Smoothing

It can be very satisfying to see the mesh when it's all smoothed out, so let's see how the TurboSmooth modifier looks with the skinning so far.

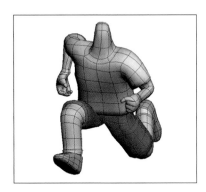

1. Apply the **TurboSmooth** modifier to the body above the Skin modifier on the stack.

2. Set **Iterations** to 1.

3. Rotate the User viewport to see the model from all angles.

4. After you've had a good look, turn off the **TurboSmooth** modifier temporarily by clicking the light bulb next to the modifier name.

5. Save the scene again as **CharSkin14.max**.

Skin Morph

When you're weighting vertices, there will be some parts of the body that don't respond correctly no matter what you do. For example, regardless of how carefully you weight the vertices at the knees (and no matter how much time you spend on them), the backs of the knees may compress unnaturally when the leg is bent at an angle of more than 75 degrees. This is a common problem with a character's joints, particularly the knees, elbows, hips, and shoulders.

To solve this problem, the Skin Morph modifier was introduced in 3ds max 7. This modifier allows you to manually pose the model to do whatever you want when a joint bends. With the knee, for example, you can go to a frame where the knee is bent, and move the vertices at the back of the knee to a more natural form.

Morph Targets and Percentages

With Skin Morph, the vertices will be unaffected when the joint is straight, but will take on the new form gradually as the knee bends. The forms you create are called *targets*. As the joint bends, the vertices will *morph* from their original form to the target form.

Morphing works with percentages of targets. When the joint is straight, the morph is at 0 percent of the target form. When the joint bends a little, the morph is triggered, and the vertices start to move toward the target. When the joint reaches the bending angle at which you created the target, the morph is at 100 percent of the form you created.

►TIP◄

The Skin modifier has angle deformer tools that perform tasks similar to what the Skin Morph modifier does. The Skin Morph modifier was introduced to make this task easier and more intuitive.

It's important to understand that the Skin Morph modifier sets its morph percentages according to the angles between bones, not by keyframes. So if you set a morph target for a bending joint, the morph target will be triggered every time the joint bends. This means you only have to set a morph target once to have it work throughout the entire animation process.

Applying Skin Morph

You apply the Skin Morph modifier above the Skin modifier on the stack. You should apply Skin Morph only after you've finished adjusting and mirroring weights with the Skin modifier. Going back to the Skin modifier after you have applied the Skin Morph modifier can produce strange results.

If there is a TurboSmooth or other smoothing modifier on the stack above the Skin modifier, you should apply the Skin Morph modifier *below* the smoothing modifier. This will reduce the number of vertices you have to move around to make targets.

Morph Bones

A morph target is always created for just two bones that are bent to a certain angle with respect to one another. In addition, the bones must be linked in a parent/child relationship.

You only have to choose the child bone when working with the Skin Morph modifier. Since every child bone has only one parent, the Skin Morph modifier will find the parent bone and determine the angle between the two bones.

Frames for Morph Targets

There are two steps in creating a morph target:

- Choose the child bone that will trigger a morph when it reaches a specific angle with respect to its parent.

- Create the morph target for that angle (move the vertices to form a better-looking joint at that angle).

It's important to perform these tasks on the appropriate frame. Performing these tasks at the wrong frame can yield strange results. But if this happens, you can delete the morph target and try again.

At the frame where you choose the child trigger bone, Skin Morph assumes that the morph target should be at 0 percent.

This means you should choose this bone at a frame where the joint is straight (usually frame 0).

You should create the morph target at a frame where the bones are at their most acute angle. Skin Morph looks at the angle of the bones at this frame, and assumes the morph target should reach 100 percent at this angle. If you've set up a test animation with a variety of movements, use a frame where the joint bends to its greatest degree.

TUTORIAL S7

Morphing the Joints

Set up Skin Morph

1. Continue from the previous exercise, or load *CharSkin14.max* from the *Skinning* folder.

2. Select the body mesh.

3. Highlight the **Skin** modifier on the stack.

   If you have TurboSmooth applied to the mesh, you'll need to apply the Skin Morph modifier below it on the stack. You can do this by choosing the *Skin* level of the stack before applying Skin Morph.

4. Apply the **Skin Morph** modifier to the mesh.

Locate the Morph Frame

1. Go to frame 30.

2. In the Left viewport, zoom in on the left knee (the back leg).

   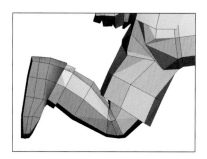

   At this frame, the knee is bent to the highest degree it's likely to achieve during the animation process. You'll use this frame to set the morph target for the knee.

3. Right-click the Left viewport label, and choose *Wireframe*.

   This will make it easier to see the morph target you're creating.

Create the Morph Target Entry

1. Unhide the bones.

2. Go to frame 0.

   At this frame, the body is in its skin pose. This is a good frame for choosing the bone that will trigger the morph.

3. Select the body mesh, and go to the **Skin Morph** level of the stack.

4. Recall that you choose the child bone when setting up a skin morph. In the Parameters rollout, click **Add Bone**, and choose **BoneCalfL**.

   This adds **BoneCalfL** to the Parameters list.

5. Highlight **BoneCalfL** on the list.

   In the Left viewport, the selected bone is indicated by a yellow bar.

6. Go to frame 30.

   This is the frame where the knee bends the most.

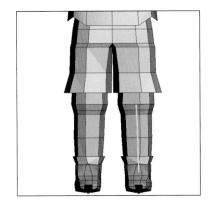

7. In the Local Properties rollout, click **Create Morph**.

   This creates a **Morph 0** listing under **BoneCalfL** on the list. The entry includes the number (100), which indicates a 100 percent morph.

8. While watching the number next to the new **Morph 0** entry on the Parameters list, scrub the time slider between frames 0 and 100.

   You can see that the morph percentage changes every time the knee bends at all. This tells you that the knee will morph to some degree every time it bends.

Form the Morph Target

When creating skin morphs, you only need the bones to be unhidden so you can select them. They don't have to be visible when you form the morph target, and are likely to get in the way at this stage.

1. Hide the bones.

2. If necessary, select the body mesh, go to the **Skin Morph** level of the stack, and highlight the **Morph 0** entry again.

3. In the Local Properties rollout, click **Edit**.

    This mode allows you to move the mesh vertices and form the morph target.

4. In the Options rollout, turn off **Show Edges**.

    This makes it easier to see what's happening with the leg.

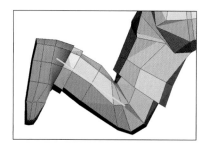

5. In the Left viewport, move the vertices at the front and back of the left knee to give it a fuller shape. You can also move the shorts' vertices to prevent them from passing through the calf.

6. Change the viewport display to *Smooth + Highlights,* and check your work. Edit the vertices further if necessary.

    You can also switch to a Right view to check the other side of the leg.

7. When you've finished working with the vertices, click the **Edit** button again to turn it off.

> **►TIP◄**
>
> It's fine to rotate the view so you can check out the leg or select vertices, but use a Left or Right view to edit vertices as often as possible. If you edit vertices in a User or Perspective view, you can easily mangle the mesh.

Finish the Morph Target

1. Scrub the time slider between 0 and 120 to watch the animation.

    The knee hasn't changed at frame 0, but it morphs partly or wholly to its edited form whenever the knee bends.

2. If you want to change the morph target some more, highlight the **Morph 0** listing in the Parameters rollout, and click **Edit** again. Move the vertices as you like. Be sure to turn off **Edit** when you've finished.

3. It's also a good idea to change the default morph target name. Highlight the **Morph 0** listing in the Parameters rollout. In the Local Properties rollout, change the name **Morph 0** to **Bend**.

4. Save the scene as **CharSkin15.max**.

> **►TIP◄**
>
> If the knee begins to morph too soon, you can make it wait until it reaches a particular angle by adjusting the **Influence Angle** parameter. The Influence Angle determines the number of degrees from the target angle at which the morph begins. For example, if the knee was bent at a 120 degree angle when you set the morph target, and the **Influence Angle** is 90, the knee will begin morphing when the bend reaches 30 degrees.

Mirroring Skin Morphs

Skin morphs can also be mirrored. Like the Skin modifier, the Skin Morph modifier mirrors the morphs using a mirror plane and threshold.

When mirroring morphs, both sides of the body must be posed symmetrically. This is why you created some symmetrical poses when you made the test animation. The vertex weights on both sides of the body should also be the same or very similar.

To mirror a skin morph, you add the mirrored bone to the list at the skin pose frame, then mirror the morph on a frame where the body is posed symmetrically at an angle similar to the one used to set the morph target.

TUTORIAL S8

Mirroring Skin Morphs

You can now mirror the skin morph you created for the left leg.

Prepare to Mirror

►TIP◄

If you try to unhide the bones using the *Bones* selection set from the main toolbar and find you can't, it's most likely because the Skin Morph modifier is at its Points sub-object level. If this occurs, you can select the Skin Morph modifier base level on the modifier stack to allow you to select the Bones set directly. You can also bypass the sub-object selection by right-clicking any viewport and choosing *Unhide by Name* from the Quad menu; you can then choose the Bones selection set from the lower right of the Unhide Objects dialog.

To mirror the morph, you'll need to add the bone to which the mirror will be applied, then mirror the morph on a frame where the legs are bent in exactly the same way.

1. Load the file *CharSkin15.max,* or continue from the previous tutorial.

2. Unhide the bones.

3. Select the body mesh, and go to the **Skin Morph** level of the stack.

4. On frame 0, click **Add Bone** and choose **BoneCalfR**.

   This adds **BoneCalfR** to the list of bones with morphs.

5. Hide the bones.

6. Go to frame 100.

   On this frame, the legs are bent exactly the same way.

7. If necessary, select the body mesh.

View the Mirroring

1. Expand the *BoneCalfL* listing in the Parameters rollout, and highlight the **Bend** morph.

2. In the Copy and Paste rollout, turn on **Show Mirror Plane** and **Preview Vertices**.

   The mirror plane is displayed as a red rectangle, and all vertices on the body appear as red. The plane should pass through the center of the body, and the mirrored vertices should be red on the opposite leg. If the mirrored vertices are not exactly on the right leg, try changing the Mirror Plane to a different axis until the vertices line up.

   If you like, you can scrub the time slider to see what the red vertices look like when the legs are not lined up. The red vertices on the right of the body always mirror the vertices on the left side. This is why you need to use a frame where the legs match. If you scrubbed the time slider, return to frame 100 before continuing.

3. In the Copy and Paste rollout, change **Mirror Threshold** to 5.0.

   Each vertex in the morph has a mirrored position on the other side that it tries to match up with a mesh vertex. The Mirror Threshold determines how far each vertex will look from its original position to find a match on the mesh.

4. In the Copy and Paste rollout, click **Paste Mirror**.

   The morph target from the left knee is copied to the right side, and a new morph target appears on the list. The two knees should now look very similar.

5. Save your work as **CharSkin16.max**.

   That's all there is to it. It takes time, but your reward is a character that animates smoothly.

6. Create skin morphs for the shoulders, elbows, buttocks, and any other areas that need them. Mirror the skin morphs as necessary.

7. For a final check, turn on the **TurboSmooth** modifier and scrub the time slider to see how the body deforms throughout the animation.

8. When you've finished creating skin morphs, save your work as **CharSkin17.max**.

TUTORIAL 59

Prepare the Rig for Animation

The last step in rigging and skinning a character is to prepare the scene for animation.

1. Load the file *CharSkin17.max*, or continue from the previous tutorial.

2. Hide all parts of the mesh.

3. Unhide the bones, and freeze them.

4. Unhide the control objects.

5. On frame 0, select all control objects.

6. Delete all the control objects' keys from the Trackbar. To do this, draw a selection region around the keys on the Trackbar (selected keys will turn white), and press **[Delete]** on the keyboard.

7. Turn on **Auto Key**.

8. On frame 1, move and rotate the wrist controls to place the character's hands at its sides.

9. Click  **Time Configuration**. Change **Start Frame** to 1, and **End Frame** to 100.

Your rig is now ready to be animated.

10. Save the scene as **CharSkinFinal.max**.

Now you're ready to enjoy the fruits of your labor. Continue on to the *Animation* section to bring the character to life.

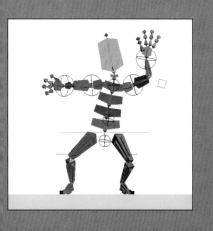

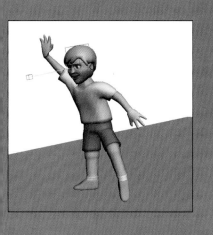

Animation

Animating a character is one of the most rewarding and entertaining things you can do with 3ds max. Your enjoyment of the process will increase as you learn more about how it's done.

I won't attempt to teach you everything there is to know about character animation—numerous books and other learning materials already cover the subject in great detail. The purpose of this section is to introduce you to the most important concepts, and to show you how to use 3ds max to animate your own characters.

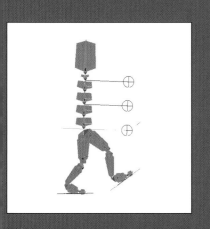

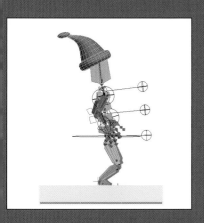

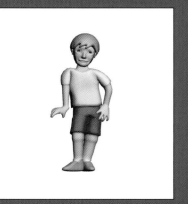

CHAPTER 6

Animating the Body

Computer-generated character animation has its roots in hand-drawn animation, with rules and principles developed in the first half of the 1900s. The approach, techniques, and terms you'll use while animating with 3ds max all come from this traditional field.

A character's body motion gives the most obvious clues to what it's doing or feeling. Through body animation, you can communicate not just action, but emotion—whether a character is happy, sad, angry, shy, loving, domineering, playful, or any other emotion or attitude.

In this book, however, we'll focus on animating the basics with 3ds max, including walking, stretching, squashing, and falling over. The art and science of making characters display emotions is too broad for the scope of this book. For further study in this area, see the resources listed at the end of this book.

Tools in 3ds max

One of the primary tools an animator has is his or her own body. When trying to figure out how to animate a particular motion or facial expression, your first course of action should be to do it yourself.

For body motions, you can do the motion slowly at first to see how your torso bends or leans, and how your limbs move. Then do the motions at normal speed to get a feel for the timing.

For facial expressions, your second-best tool is a mirror. Make the faces yourself, and note how your facial muscles and features respond to each emotion.

Professional animators use these tools daily. Be sure to use them yourself!

You've already used some of 3ds max's animation tools when you created the test animation in Chapter 5. Here, we'll go into more depth on these tools and how they work.

Keys

Creating a basic animation with 3ds max is easy—you turn on **Auto Key**, move the time slider to a frame later than 0, and move, rotate, or scale objects.

Each time you do this, 3ds max creates a *key* at the current frame. That frame then becomes a *keyframe*. When you play the animation, 3ds max figures out the action in between the keyframes. In other words, 3ds max *interpolates* the animation between keys (you may also hear it referred to as 'tweening').

There are a number of ways in 3ds max to set and change keys, and to change the way the animation interpolates between keys. Your primary tools for working with keys are the Trackbar and the Track View windows.

> ▶TIP◀
>
> The term *key* comes from hand-drawn animation. An expert animator would draw only the key (most important) frames in an animated sequence, then hand them off to a junior animator to fill in the frames in between.

Trackbar

The Trackbar is located below the time slider. When you create a key, a red rectangle appears on the Trackbar at that frame number to indicate that there's a key there. It doesn't tell you whether it's a position, rotation, or scale key, or whether one of the object's parameters has been animated. It simply tells you that there's a key of some kind at that frame.

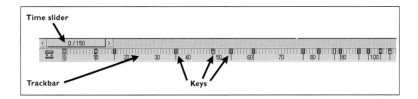

The Trackbar also shows the *active time segment*, which is the number of frames currently available in the animation. You can change the active time segment by clicking ⌧ **Time Configuration** at the lower right of the screen and changing the **Length** parameter in the Time Configuration dialog.

The Trackbar is useful for simple edits such as moving or copying keys to change the animation's timing. In the next tutorial, you'll learn to use the Trackbar to copy and edit keys. If you already know how to use the Trackbar, you can skip the next tutorial.

TUTORIAL A1
Working with Keys

In this tutorial, you'll animate a character making a few simple motions. You'll also adjust the animation using the Trackbar and other keyframing tools.

Animate a Waving Arm

When you pose the arm and hand for a waving motion, they'll look very strange at first. You must keep the final

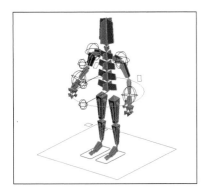

►TIP◄

If you didn't do the rigging tutorials, take a few moments to play with the controls and get a feel for what they do. Before continuing with this exercise, be sure to undo any movements or rotations you make, or reload the file *CharAnimRig.max*.

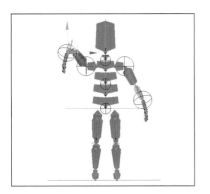

►TIP◄

It will be easier for you to rotate the control objects with the Local coordinate system because the rotation gizmo's axes will always correspond to the hand's orientation.

goal in mind, and follow through with all the steps to complete the pose.

1. Load the file *CharSkinFinal.max* that you saved at the end of the chapter, or load the file *CharAnimRig.max* from the *Animation/Scenes* folder on the CD.

   This scene contains a character rig, ready to be animated. You can animate the character by moving and rotating the controls at the shoulders, wrists, spine, and feet. The bones have been frozen so you won't select them by accident.

2. Click ⊡ **Time Configuration**. Change **Start Time** to 1 and **End Time** to 100. Click **OK** to set the new segment length.

   This will start the animation with the character in a more realistic pose.

3. Go to frame 10 by pulling the time slider, or by entering the number 10 in the frame number entry area at the lower right of the screen.

   If you enter the frame number manually, be sure to press [**Enter**].

4. Turn on **Auto Key**.

5. In the Front viewport, raise the right wrist control so it's at roughly the same height as the character's neck.

   This will make the elbow and hand look very strange. Don't worry, just keep going!

6. Click ↻ **Select and Rotate**, and choose the **Local** coordinate system.

7. Rotate the wrist control until the palm faces away from the character, as if it were waving hello.

8. In the Top viewport, move the wrist control in front of the body a little to make the pose more natural.

Lower the Hand

On frame 20, you want the character to put its hand back by its side. There's already a key for this pose on frame 1, so you'll simply copy the key from frame 1 to 20.

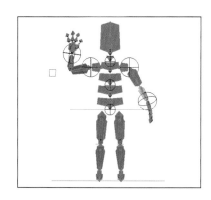

1. Go to frame 20.

2. Select the right wrist control, if it's not already selected.

3. On the Trackbar, select the key at frame 1 by clicking it.

   The key turns white to indicate that it's selected.

4. Hold down **[Shift]**, and move the key from frame 1 to 20.

   The character's wrist returns to its rest position.

5. Drag the time slider, scrubbing between frames 1 and 20, to watch the character wave—your first animation.

Wave the Left Arm

Now we want the character to wave its other arm.

1. Go to frame 30.

2. Move and rotate the character's left wrist control to make the left arm wave hello.

3. Pull the time slider between frames 1 and 30 to see the animation.

   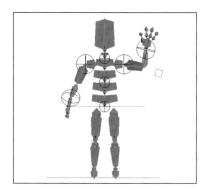

   There's a problem here. The left arm starts moving at frame 1, rather than staying still until frame 20. This is because there's no key for the left arm at frame 20, so the program is interpolating between the only two keys you've set for this object, at frames 1 and 30.

   To solve this problem, you can copy the left wrist key from frame 1 to 20. When 3ds max interpolates between these keys, there will be no in-between motion because the keys will be exactly the same.

4. With the left arm control selected, hold down **[Shift]** and drag the key at frame 1 to frame 20 to copy it.

5. Pull the time slider again. The character's left arm stays still until frame 20, then starts moving.

    The problem you just solved is a common one when animating with 3ds max. The program simply interpolates from one key to the next. If you want a body part to stay still for a certain period of time, you must set a key to tell it to do so.

6. Let's copy another key to make the arm come back down at frame 40. Copy the key at frame 20 to frame 40.

7. On frame 25, adjust the left arm to a more natural intermediate pose, and copy this key to frame 35.

8. Play the animation.

    Now the character raises its right arm and puts it down, then raises its left arm and puts it down.

9. Save the scene as **CharAnimWave01.max**.

Bend the Knees

Next, you'll make the character bend its knees. To do this, you can simply select **CtrlLegs** (the circle around the hips) and move it downward. But suppose you want the character to keep its knees straight until frame 40, then bend its knees at frame 50. You'll need to set a key for **CtrlLegs** at frame 40 to keep it from moving until that point. This time, let's try a different method for copying keys.

1. Select **CtrlLegs**, the circle at the hips.

2. At any frame, right-click the time slider.

    The Create Key dialog appears.

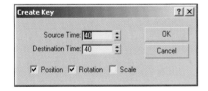

3. In the Create Key dialog, leave **Position** and **Rotation** turned on, and turn off **Scale**.

    You'll only ever animate the position and rotation of your control objects, so you only have to copy these keys.

4. Set the **Source Time** and **Destination Time** to 40, and click **OK**.

   This sets a key for **CtrlLegs** at frame 40. There's no key at frame 1, which is just fine.

5. Go to frame 50.

6. In the Front viewport, move **CtrlLegs** downward to bend the knees.

   Now you want the character to come back up on frame 60.

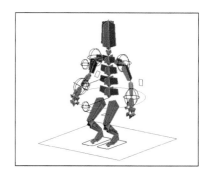

7. Copy the key at frame 40 to frame 60 using either of the methods you now know.

8. Play the animation.

   After raising each arm, the character bends its knees, then stands up again.

9. Save the scene as **CharAnimWave02.max**.

Walk Cycle

A *walk cycle* is exactly that: A cycle of motion for making a character walk. It's called a *cycle* because it can be repeated over and over again. The walk cycle is part of any professional character animator's bag of tricks.

Before you animate a walk cycle, get up and study how you actually walk. Use these questions as a guide to help you figure out what makes up a walk:

- Start from a standing position, with your feet under your shoulders. When you want to start walking, what's the first thing you do?

- How far forward do you place your stepping foot from the one behind?

- What is the foot in the back doing while you step?

- Does the foot in front bend? How about the back foot?

- Are your knees bent or straight?

> **►TIP◄**
>
> Walking is so natural for most of us that it can be hard to determine what your body is doing. You can get a better feel for what's actually going on by exaggerating your motions a little bit.

- Are you taller when one foot is in the air, or when both feet are on the ground?

- What are your hips doing while you walk? It can be helpful to put a hand on the side of one hip and see if you can feel any shifts as you move.

- Now swing your arms a little while you walk. Do they match your legs, or do they move opposite your legs?

- What do your shoulders do as you swing your arms?

The answers to these questions will help you animate a walk cycle more effectively.

The Set Key System

When animating a walk cycle, you'll be setting keys for many parts of the rig at regular intervals. It would be very tedious if you had to keep checking to see where the last key was set for each body part, and copying keys to keep body parts from moving.

An alternative tool for setting keys is the Set Key system. With this system, you can set (create) a key for several objects with just one mouse click. This saves you the trouble of going back later and copying keys to keep objects from moving. The Set Key system is ideal for setting up cycles of motion, such as a walk cycle.

The controls used in the Set Key system are located at the lower right of the screen, just below the end of the Trackbar. Before using the Set Key system, you'll need to create a selection set that includes all the objects for which you want to set keys. In addition, you must use the Key Filters tool to specify the tracks for which you want to set keys.

When the Set Key **Set Key** button is turned on, you can click ⊶ **Set Keys** to set keys for filtered tracks on objects in the selection set at that frame.

The Set Key system is particularly useful for roughing out an animation sequence. For example, animators often rough out a scene by setting keys at regular intervals, such as every 5 or 10 frames. The Set Key system makes this process very fast.

Afterward, the animator moves or deletes keys to adjust the timing. For that task, the Auto Key system described earlier works better.

► TIP ◄

Animators use the term *roughing out* to describe the process of quickly placing keys at approximate times. The result, a *rough sequence*, gives the animator an idea of how the motion will flow and often provides the basis for the final animation.

TUTORIAL A2

Creating a Walk Cycle

Before you start animating a walk cycle, let's take a look at a completed walk cycle to see how it's keyframed.

Load a Completed Walk Cycle

1. Load the file *CharAnimWalk.max* from the *Animation/Scenes* folder on the CD.

   This scene contains an example of a walk cycle.

2. Play the animation.

   The character walks forward slowly, taking a step on each foot. Its final pose is the same as its starting pose, but in a different location in the scene.

   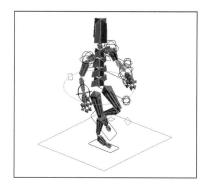

   In this animation, the keys have been set every 10 frames. Let's take a closer look at the keyframes.

3. Go to frame 0, and study the pose.

   The character has one foot in the air, and is standing nearly straight.

4. Scrub the time slider slowly from frame 0 to frame 10.

   The character puts its right foot forward, just barely reaching the ground as it leans forward.

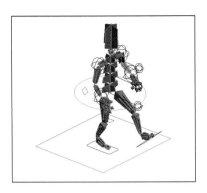

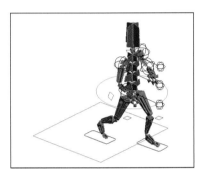

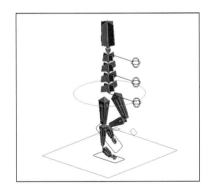

5. Scrub the time slider to frame 20.

    The character shifts its weight from the back foot to the front foot.

6. Scrub the time slider to frame 30.

    The character is posed in a mirror image of the pose at frame 0, this time with its left foot in the air.

7. Scrub the time slider to frame 60.

    The character repeats the same motions with the other foot.

8. Now play the animation while watching it in the Front viewport.

    As the character steps onto one leg, it shifts its weight from one side to the other.

Prepare the Scene for Set Key

Now you're ready to animate your own walk cycle using the Set Key system.

1. Load *CharAnimWalkLegs01.max* from the *Animation/Scenes* folder on the CD.

    This file contains a simplified rig to make it easier for you to practice making a walk cycle. The rig is posed at frame 0 in the *passing position*, where one foot is in the air, ready to take a step.

    To use the Set Key system, you'll need a selection set that includes all objects for which you want to set keys. In this instance, all the control objects. That selection set, called *Control Objects*, already exists.

2. At the lower right of the screen, just above the Key Filters button, choose the selection set *Control Objects* from the list.

    Now you must indicate for which of those objects' tracks you want to set keys.

3. Click **Key Filters**. In the Set Key Filters dialog, turn on **Position**, **Rotation**, and **Custom Attributes**, and turn off all other options. Close the dialog by clicking the **[X]** at its upper-right corner.

4. Turn on the Set Key **Set Key** button.

   The button turns red to indicate it's on.

5. Go to frame 0.

6. Click 🔑 **Set Keys**.

   This sets a key for all the control objects at the current frame.

►TIP◄

If you pose the character, then go to another frame before clicking **Set Keys**, you'll lose the pose you just created.

Animate the First Leg Pose

Now you can start animating the legs to make the character walk.

1. Go to frame 10.

2. In Left viewport, move **CtrlLegs** (the circle at the hips) down and to the right, and rotate it slightly to make the character lean forward.

   The rig will look strange while you're posing it. This is normal.

3. Move and rotate the left foot control to pose the character in mid-stepping motion.

4. Click 🔑 **Set Keys**.

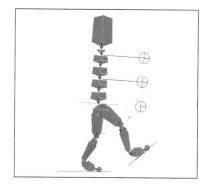

Animate the Stepping Pose

Animating the rest of the walk cycle is as simple as creating more poses and setting keys for them.

1. Go to frame 20.

2. In the Left viewport, move **CtrlLegs** slightly up and to the right.

3. Rotate the left foot to step flat on the ground, and move it so it's at the same height as the right foot.

4. Choose *Animation > Parameter Collector* to open the Parameter Collector, and set **RollR** to 65.

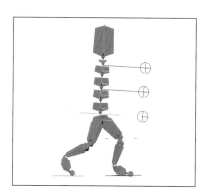

5. Move **CtrlKneeR** forward (in the direction of the walk) to make the right knee bend correctly.

6. Click 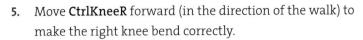 **Set Keys**.

Animate the Passing Position

1. Go to frame 30.

2. In the Left viewport, move **CtrlLegs** up and to the right, so the left leg is nearly straight. Rotate **CtrlLegs** to make the character stand up straight.

3. In the Parameter Collector, change **RollR** to 0, and move and rotate the right foot into the passing position.

4. Click  **Set Keys**.

5. Scrub the time slider between frames 0 and 30 to see the animation so far. If the animation looks wrong, look back over the steps to see which pose is incorrect. Fix the pose, and click **Set Keys**.

   If the back leg appears to straighten then jerk forward around frame 20, you can move **CtrlLegs** down a little on frame 20 to bend the knees more. Be sure to click **Set Keys** after making this change.

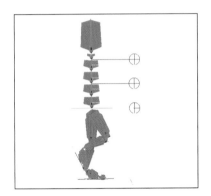

Animate the Remaining Poses

The rest of the walk is a repeat of the first part, but with the right leg stepping forward instead of the left. Use the pictures as a guide when setting the remainder of the poses.

1. Go to frame 40. Move and rotate the right foot in the stepping position. Move **CtrlLegs** forward slightly, and rotate it to make the character lean forward. Click 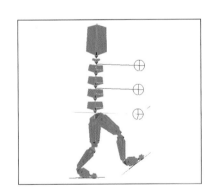 **Set Keys**.

2. On frame 50, move **CtrlLegs** slightly forward and up. On the Parameter Collector, change **RollL** to 65, and move **CtrlKneeL** forward to make the left knee bend correctly. Click 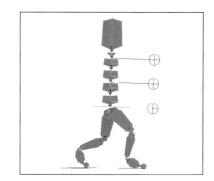 **Set Keys**.

3. On frame 60, bring the left foot up into the passing position and set **RollR** back to 0. Move **CtrlLegs** to straighten out the right leg, and rotate it to straighten up the spine. Click 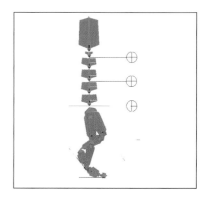 **Set Keys**.

4. Scrub the time slider between frames 0 and 60 to see the animation.

Balance the Character

The walk is coming along. But if you watch the animation in the Front viewport, you'll see that the character isn't balanced. When it's on one leg, its entire weight should be centered over the standing leg.

1. Go to frame 0. In the Front viewport, move **CtrlLegs** to the left to center the spine over the right leg. Click **Set Keys**.

   On frame 10, the character is about to place its foot on the ground. Here, its weight is almost centered over the two legs, but not quite.

2. On frame 10, in the Front viewport, move **CtrlLegs** slightly to the left, and click **Set Keys**.

   On frames 20 and 50, the character's weight is balanced between both legs. This is appropriate for this pose because both feet are on the ground, so you don't have to change the pose on these frames.

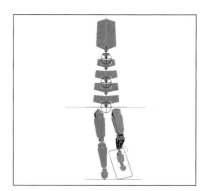

3. On frame 30, move **CtrlLegs** to the right to center the spine over the left foot, and click **Set Keys**.

4. On frame 40, move **CtrlLegs** slightly to the right, and click **Set Keys**.

5. On frame 60, move **CtrlLegs** to the left to balance the character over its right leg.

   You have now created a basic walk cycle.

6. Save the scene as **CharAnimWalkLegs02**.max.

   If you like, you can unhide the arm bones and controls, and animate the arms swinging opposite the legs.

Track View

Track View is like the Trackbar on steroids. It's a comprehensive chart where you can find information on every key on every object. With Track View, you can change the animation's timing, loop the animation, change the interpolation between keys, and much more.

Track View has two display modes: the Dope Sheet and the Curve Editor. The Dope Sheet displays all keys as dots, the Curve Editor shows the interpolation between keys as curves. Each has its own uses.

The Dope Sheet shows each key on each track as a separate dot. You can click a key to find out its value, and change it right in the Track View window. To access the Dope Sheet, choose *Graph Editors menu > Track View > Dope Sheet*.

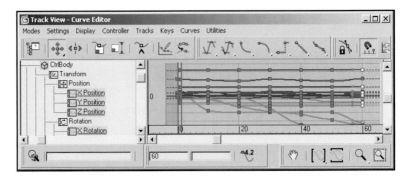

The Curve Editor shows you each animation track as a set of curves connecting the keys, representing the interpolation between the keys. You can't really tell what the animation looks like by looking at a curve, but you can spot problem areas by looking for spikes or other odd shapes in the curve. You can also change the shape of the curve, which will change the default interpolation between keys.

The Curve Editor is also where you loop animation. When you loop a sequence of keys, 3ds max continues the curves for the remainder of the animation duration and shows them in the Curve Editor. This makes it easy to how the animation flows throughout the active time segment.

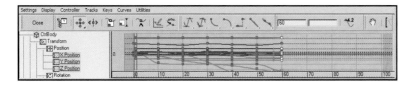

To access the Curve Editor, choose *Graph Editors > Track View > Curve Editor*. You can also access a miniature version of the Curve Editor by clicking the ☒ **Mini Curve Editor (Toggle)** button at the left end of the Trackbar. This is just a smaller version of the Curve Editor, with fewer tools.

TUTORIAL A3

Looping Animation

In this tutorial, you'll loop a simple walk cycle using the Curve Editor.

Prepare the Scene

1. Load *CharAnimLoop01.max* from the *Animation/Scenes* folder on the CD.

2. Play the animation.

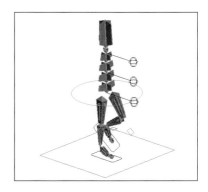

This is a version of the walk cycle you created in the last tutorial. The only difference is that the keyframes on frame 0 have been deleted to make looping easier. You're going to loop this walk cycle using Track View, then use Track View again to spot and solve problems with the animation.

3. To see the looped animation, you'll need more frames. Click ⬜ **Time Configuration**, and set **Length** to 300.

Loop the Keyframes

1. Select all the control objects. Since the bones are frozen, you can select all the control objects by drawing a selection region around the entire character.

2. Choose *Graph Editors > Track View > Curve Editor*.

In the Curve Editor, you can see a series of curves. All the curves for all the selected objects are shown at the same time. When you work with the curves later, you'll work with them one at a time.

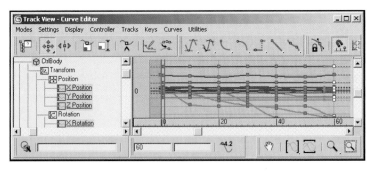

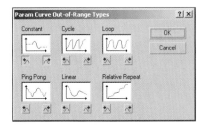

3. On the Track View toolbar, click ⬜ **Parameter Curve Out-of-Range Types**.

The Parameter Curve Out-of-Range Types dialog appears. You use this dialog to specify what the animation should do when it goes beyond the currently set keys. By default, the out-of-range parameter curve is set to **Constant**.

In this animation, keys have been set on frames 1 through 60. This means the animation stays the same after it reaches frame 60. You can see in the Curve Editor that each curve turns into a straight, dotted line after frame 60.

4. On the Parameter Curve Out-of-Range Types dialog, click the right arrow under **Relative Repeat**.

    Relative Repeat is a type of looping where the animation repeats, but with the new initial position determined by the last keyframe. If you had selected **Loop** instead, the character would keep going back to its original location and starting all over again.

5. Click **OK** to close the Parameter Curve Out-of-Range Types dialog, but leave Track View open for now.

6. Play the animation.

    The character walks and walks and walks.

Loop Custom Attributes

The character is walking, but the custom attributes aren't looping. You'll have to loop these parameters separately.

1. Select the left foot control.

2. In the Curve Editor hierarchy, expand the listing for **CtrlFootL** to show *Object (Rectangle)* > *Custom Attributes* > *RollL*, and highlight **RollL**.

3. On the Track View toolbar, click ▦ **Parameter Curve Out-of-Range Types**. Click the right arrow under **Relative Repeat**, and click **OK** to close the dialog.

4. Select the right foot control, and perform the same steps for the **RollR** parameter.

5. Play the animation.

    Now the feet roll and unroll as the character walks.

Fix a Looping Curve

If you study the looped animation closely in frames 250–300, you will find some problems that become apparent around this time. The right foot becomes more and more tilted as the animation goes on, the legs become much straighter, and the hips lean to one side.

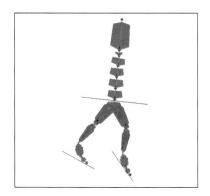

Such problems indicate that the keys on one or more objects don't match on the first and last frames. Any slight offset is compounded each time the animation loops, so the problem becomes obvious only after it has looped several times.

In particular, the tilted right foot indicates that the rotation of **CtrlFootR** doesn't match on the first and last keyframes. The straightening legs and leaning hips tell you there's a problem with **CtrlLegs**, where its X and Z axis values don't match on the first and last keyframes. You'll fix these problems with Track View.

1. Select **CtrlLegs**.

2. In the Curve Editor, click **X Position** for **CtrlLegs**.

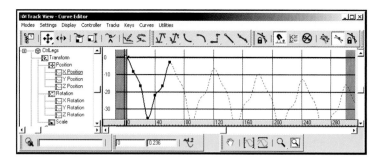

Now you can see just the curve for this track. You can clearly see that the curve for the X position gradually sinks down, indicating that the first and last keyframes don't match.

3. Click the first key dot on the curve.

    At the bottom of the Curve Editor are two entry areas. One shows the keyframe number, which is 0. The other shows the value of the key. In this case, the value is -21.891.

4. Click the last key on the curve, at frame 60.

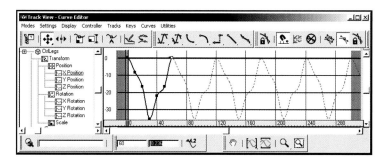

5. In the value entry area, enter –21.891, then press [Enter].

   The curve now shows the animation looping perfectly, with the curve following the same pattern at all times without gradually going higher or lower.

Fix the Remaining Curves

1. Highlight the **Z Position** listing for **CtrlLegs**.

   The curve for the Z value gradually rises.

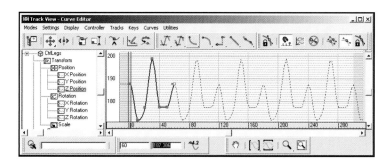

2. Click the dot on the curve at frame 0 to get the value of the key, then click the dot at frame 60 and enter the value.

3. Locate the **Rotation** tracks for **CtrlFootR**, and use the same technique to fix each rotation curve.

4. Correct any other tracks that look like they need work. In general, all Position and Rotation tracks except Y Position should loop evenly. The Y Position track will change over time because the control objects are moving steadily in that direction.

> ▶TIP◀
>
> You can copy a key value from one entry area with [Ctrl-C] and paste it into another with [Ctrl-V]. Be sure to press [Enter] after pasting the value.

5. Correct the looping for **CtrlKneeL** and **CtrlKneeR**. These control objects get farther away from the character with each step. To keep them from moving too far away, go to a late frame in the animation such as 250 or 300, and in the Curve Editor, select the last set of keys that have the same value. Move these keys up or down in the graph to see the control objects move toward and away from the character.

6. When you've finished correcting curves, play the animation. If you see any more errors, see if you can spot the control object that's causing the trouble, and check its curves in the Curve Editor.

7. When you're satisfied with the animation, save the scene as **CharAnimLoop02.max**.

Animation Principles

Once upon a time, there was a little studio called the Walt Disney Company. From the 1920s to the 1960s, founder Walt Disney and his crew of animators practically invented the field of animation. The principles they discovered and the terminology they used persist to this day, even in the field of computer-generated animation.

Here, we'll look at the principles of animation developed at the Disney studios, which are still in constant use by the best character animators today. Then we'll explore ways to implement these rules in 3ds max.

"But," you say, "they were drawing each frame by hand. I'm using a computer. Surely the rules are different!" Not true. Only the way we put the rules into practice has changed: Computers have taken over a lot of the repetitive tasks. However, to make an animation that an audience will want to watch, you'll need to know these important rules, and how to use them in your own work.

- **EXAGGERATION** Truly entertaining animation doesn't just mimic real life, it exaggerates it. Whatever the character is doing, show it large.

- **TIMING** This refers to the amount of time an action takes. In general, some of your actions will have to be timed like real-life motions so the audience knows what's going on. For actions that are fast or slow in real life, exaggerate the timing. This means fast actions should be very fast, and slow actions should be even slower.

►TIP◄

To calculate timing, you'll need to know the frame rate of your final animation. For example, if an action should take half a second and you're animating at 30 frames per second (fps), then the action should be 15 frames long.

- **SQUASH AND STRETCH** Animated characters can be bent, stretched, and squashed into all kinds of positions. Use squash and stretch to exaggerate motion, to make the character double over into a curled position, or stretch its torso, arms, and legs into athletic leaps.

- **ANTICIPATION AND FOLLOW-THROUGH** Before the character takes action, show an anticipatory motion just before so the audience knows something's about to happen. After the action, show the results of the action.

- **OVERLAPPING ACTION** The character should always be doing at least two things at once. For example, if he's waving his arms, he could stand on tiptoe to get attention, or look around wildly for help.

- **SECONDARY MOTION** If the character is wearing a hat or some loose clothing, or has a long appendage such as a tail, these should be animated separately to respond to the character's motion.

- **ARCS** Move body parts in arcs, not straight lines.

- **STAGING** Avoid having both sides of the character's body posed identically, and keep the character moving at all times.

►TIP◄

Certain animated television shows have elected to reduce animation costs by letting some of these principles slide. Usually, the first principle to go is "keep the character moving at all times." Can you think of any of these shows?

These principles should be used in all your character animation, regardless of the tools you use to create it.

Learning to Use the Principles

One of the best ways to study how these principles are used in practice is to look at as many professional productions as possible.

Here are some ideas for how to improve your own abilities to use these principles:

- Watch animated films and television shows with the sound turned off. This works equally well with traditional 2D- and 3D-animated shows and movies. See how many of the principles you can spot.

- Go to Web sites that feature professional 3D animation. Animators seeking work frequently post their *demo reels* (work samples) on these sites. The advantage of looking at animation online is that you often have the opportunity to email the artist with questions about his or her work.

- Show your work-in-progress to others. The animation process has been collaborative since its earliest days, and even seasoned veterans will ask another animator for an opinion or idea. When it comes to helping beginners, I'm constantly surprised by how willing the pros are to offer constructive critiques. Of course, you shouldn't make a pest of yourself; work for the best quality you can before seeking a critique.

In the next tutorial, you will explore how to use the animation principles in practice with 3ds max.

TUTORIAL A4

Animating an Action Sequence

In this exercise, you'll load a simple animation that contains just a few keyframes, and use the principles of animation to improve it.

Load the Scene

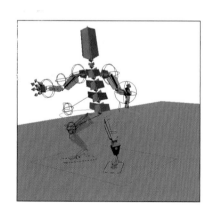

1. Load *CharAnimCatch01.max* from the *Animation/Scenes* folder on the CD, and play the animation.

   This scene contains a brief animation of a character being hit by a ball. Not very good, is it?

2. Look at the list of animation principles and see if you can spot what's missing.

Is the timing good? How could it be improved? Is there any anticipation or follow-through?

Adjust the Action Timing

You can easily tighten up the timing of the hit from the ball by moving the keys on the Trackbar.

1. Select all the objects in the scene, including the ball, and look at the Trackbar.

2. Move the keys closer together so they're only two or three frames apart.

3. Move all the keys so the first one occurs around frame 60.

4. Play the animation again.

The action is better, but the sequence still needs work.

Add Anticipation

The character isn't doing anything before he gets hit by the ball. Let's give it some anticipatory motions. To rough out the motion, you'll use the Set Key system.

1. At the bottom right of the screen, select the *Control Objects* selection set.

2. Click **Key Filters**, and turn on **Position, Rotation,** and **Custom Attributes.** Turn off all other options, and close the dialog.

3. Turn on [Set Key] **Set Key.**

4. Exaggerate the pose as much as you like. Click [⊶] **Set Keys.**

Don't forget to pose the clavicles and spine.

5. On frame 10 or 15, put the character in a different pose. You can lean the spine in a different direction, or move **CtrlLegs** to shift the character's weight. Click [⊶] **Set Keys** to set the pose.

6. Set up four or five more poses, until the last pose you set is 10–15 frames away from the character's pose when it gets hit by the ball.

7. Turn off **Set Key**.

Remove the Twins

In the animation industry, a character that's posed identically on both sides is referred to as *twins*. Twins are considered bad form in character animation because they're boring. If a pose is boring, it shouldn't be part of your animation!

The frame where the character gets hit by the ball has a twins pose. You can fix this easily by varying the character in some way.

1. Turn on **Auto Key**.

2. On the frame where the character gets hit by the ball, vary the pose by moving **CtrlLegs** to shift its weight, by tilting the spine, or by moving one or both of its hands.

Add Follow-Through

The animation now has anticipation and better staging. Now, we'll add some follow-through motions. When the character hits the ground, it just lies there. Let's add some overlapping motion to make the follow-through more interesting.

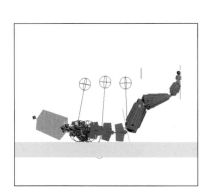

1. On the frame where the character hits the ground, move its feet up a bit in the Left viewport.

2. Go to a frame 3–4 frames later. In the Left viewport, move **CtrlLegs** up a bit.

3. A few frames later, move **CtrlLegs** back down.

4. Play the animation.

   Now the character anticipates the hit, and bounces a little when it lands.

5. Work with the timing of the motions until you are satisfied with the animation.

If you like, you can unhide the mesh and render the animation.

6. Save the scene as **CharAnimCatch02.max**.

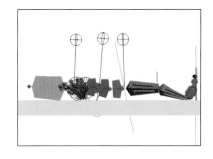

This tutorial gave you an idea of how you can implement the principles of animation when working with 3ds max. In practice, you would work with the timing and motions a great deal more before pronouncing the animation finished.

To see two other versions of the animation, load the files *Char-AnimCatch02.max* and *CharAnimCatch03.max* from the CD. You'll also find a rendered animation, *CharAnimCatch05.avi*, in the *Animation/AVI* folder on the CD.

Modifiers and Controllers

There are several modifiers and controllers in 3ds max that you can use to implement the principles of animation.

Modifiers

Modifiers are designed to be applied to mesh objects. Usually (but not always), you'll apply these modifiers to non-skinned objects. These would include the head and any ancillary objects, such as a hat or antennae.

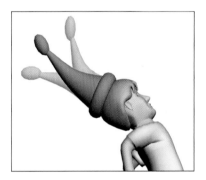

- **FLEX** This modifier adds secondary motion by making the model respond automatically to movement. You can use it to make a hat or antennae bounce around, or to make a big belly jiggle.

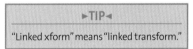
►TIP◄
"Linked xform" means "linked transform."

- **LINKED XFORM** You can use this modifier to link specific vertices or other sub-objects to another object. If you animate the parent objects, the sub-objects will also animate.

- **SQUASH AND STRETCH** These modifiers make objects deform by squashing and stretching.

- **MORPHER** You can use the Morpher modifier to *morph* (gradually change) between different mesh objects with the same number of vertices. This technique is particularly useful for animating facial expressions and speech. You'll learn more about this modifier in the next chapter.

Rather than use modifiers, you might be tempted use the Scale transforms on the main toolbar to animate objects squashing and stretching. However, this will create problems in your animation. The Scale transforms don't work well with linked objects, so you should avoid using them in character animation.

Controllers

Controllers (also known as *constraints*) can also be used to animate the character.

- **NOISE CONTROLLER** This controller can give an object random movement.

- **LINK CONSTRAINT** You can use the link constraint to cause an object to be linked to different objects on different frames.

TUTORIAL A5

Animating with Modifiers and Controllers

In this tutorial, you'll use a link constraint and Linked XForm modifier to animate a scene.

Load the Scene

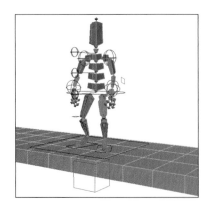

1. Load the file *CharAnimLanding01.max* from the *Animation/Scenes* folder on the CD.

    This file contains a plank, a dummy object, and a character rig. The rig in this scene has been set up slightly differently from the rig you've been using. All the control objects are rigged with wiring and expressions rather than reactions. The control objects are similar to what you're accustomed to using, with custom attributes on the wrists and feet.

2. Play the animation.

    The character lands on the plank around frame 25. The dummy object moves up and down after the character lands.

Apply a Linked Xform Modifier

The dummy object has been animated to simulate a *stagger* effect. This is a traditional animation effect where an object moves back and forth less and less over a series of frames, then finally comes to rest. You'll use the dummy object and a Linked Xform modifier to animate the plank wobbling as the character lands on it.

1. Select the plank, and add a **Mesh Select** modifier to it.

2. At the 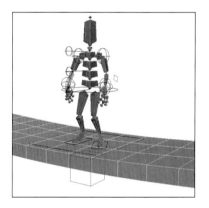 **Vertex** sub-object level, select the two rows of vertices just above the dummy object.

3. In the Soft Selection rollout, turn on **Use Soft Selection**, and set **Falloff** to about 1250.

   This will extend the soft selection nearly to the ends of the plank.

4. Without exiting the **Vertex** sub-object level, apply a **Linked XForm** modifier to the plank.

5. Click **Pick Control Object**, and click the dummy object.

6. Play the animation.

   The plank now wobbles when the character lands on it. Its vertices follow the dummy object, with a lesser effect at the ends of the plank according to the soft selection.

Assign a Link Constraint

After the character lands on the plank, its body should move up and down to match the motion of the plank. You can create this effect by linking the body control to the dummy object.

You really only want the body to follow the dummy object after it lands. You can use a link constraint to cause the body control to link to the dummy object only at a specific frame.

1. Go to frame 30.

2. Select **CtrlBody**.

3. Choose *Animation > Constraints > Link Constraints,* and click the dummy object.

On the **Motion** panel, you can see the Link Params rollout. It shows you that the link to the dummy object **Dummy Bounce** begins on frame 30.

4. Play the animation.

    Now the character follows the motion of the plank as the plank bends.

5. Save the scene as **CharAnimLanding02.max**.

Animate Squash and Stretch

►TIP◄

The Selection Filter is at the left side of the main toolbar. By default, it is set to **All**.

Now you must animate the character squashing and stretching after the landing. You won't actually squash or stretch the body mesh, but will use exaggerated poses to suggest squashing and stretching.

1. Set the **Selection Filter** to *Shapes*.

2. Turn on **Auto Key**.

3. On frame 30, select all the control objects. Right-click the time slider, and set a **Position** and **Rotation** key for all selected objects at this frame.

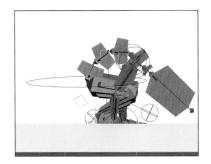

4. On frame 38, move and rotate the control objects to pose the character in a curled position.

    This will simulate an exaggerated pose after a hard landing.

5. On frame 44, straighten up the character and make him arch back a little.

6. On frame 48, curl him over a little.

7. Pose the character a few more times, alternating between curling and arching the character every few frames. You can also scrub to intermediate frames and make any corrections necessary.

8. After the character comes to rest, have him look around to the right and left. Be sure to animate the character's head turning in an arc, where the neck and head swing forward slightly as he turns.

To quickly jump from keyframe to keyframe, you can turn on the 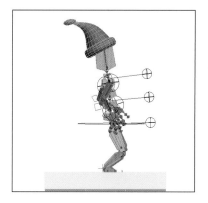 Key Mode Toggle at the bottom right of the screen. This causes the **Previous Frame** and **Next Frame** buttons to become the ◄ **Previous Key** and ►| **Next Key** buttons. You can use these buttons to jump from one key to the next for the selected object.

Add the Flex Modifier

1. Unhide the object **Hat**.

   This hat is currently linked to **BoneHead**. It animates with the character, but it's very stiff. You'll use the **Flex** modifier to make it flop around in response to the motion.

2. At frame 0, zoom in on the hat in the Left viewport, and select the vertices that make up the pom-pom at the top of the hat.

3. Turn on **Use Soft Selection**, and increase the **Falloff** value until it reaches about three-fourths of the way down the hat.

4. While still at the **Vertex** sub-object level, apply the **Flex** modifier to the hat.

5. Scrub the time slider to see the result.

   If the hat flops around too much, try decreasing the **Flex** value on the Parameters rollout to a lower value such as 0.1 or 0.3.

6. Save the scene as **CharAnimLanding03.max**.

   You can find a finished version of this scene in the file *CharAnimLanding04.max*, and in the rendered animation *CharAnimLanding05.avi* in the *Animation/AVI* folder on the CD. This file has motion blur applied to the character mesh and the plank to make the motion look smoother.

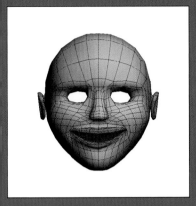

CHAPTER 7

Facial Animation

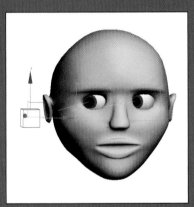

Although you can go a long way toward completing a scene simply by animating the character's body, animating the character's face adds greatly to the expressiveness of a sequence. At the very least, you'll want the character to blink its eyes. You can also animate the character to look around and react to its circumstances with various facial expressions. And you can animate its mouth to make it speak in sync with a soundtrack.

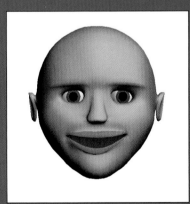

Eye Animation

One of the easiest ways to breathe more life into an animation is to make the eyes look in various directions during the sequence.

Look-At Constraint

To control the eyes, you can use a *look-at constraint*. This forces the eyes to always follow a control object somewhere in front of the head, called the *look-at target*. Making the eyes look in different directions then becomes a simple matter of moving the look-at target.

To use this tool, you will need to create separate objects for the eyeballs. Usually, you'll start with spheres, and change their shapes slightly to fit the facial model.

FFD Space Warp

When you use a look-at constraint, the eyes rotate to look at the target. If they aren't perfectly spherical, the eyes will look strange when they rotate.

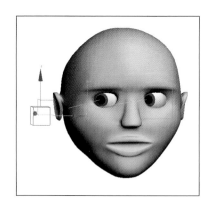

To solve this problem, you can use a *free form deformation* (FFD) tool. This creates a lattice around an object, and you can move the points on the lattice to deform the object. Then, when you use a look-at constraint, the eyes will stay deformed according to the lattice as they rotate to face the look-at target.

There are several FFD tools in 3ds max. For the eyes, you'll use an FFD *space warp*. A space warp is similar to a modifier, but it shapes the object using a separate gizmo that can stay put while the object moves or rotates. This means the space warp always applies the same deformation to the object regardless of whether the object is animated.

The FFD space warp will keep the eyeball conformed to the head while the eye rotates to face the look-at target.

Animating the Eyes

In this tutorial, you'll shape the eyeballs to fit the head, then add a look-at constraint so you can animate them looking in different directions.

Try out a Look-At Constraint

1. Load the file *CharAnimEyes01.max* from the *Animation/ Scenes* folder on the CD.

   This scene contains a head similar to the one you created in Chapter 2, and a dummy object placed a short distance from the head. You'll use this object as the look-at target for the eyes.

   We'll use this scene because the head has been frozen to prevent you from accidentally selecting it. Also, the eyes were created as separate spheres, then converted to Editable Poly objects, and shaped by scaling vertices at the Vertex sub-object level. The pupils were given a different material ID so the pupils and whites can have different colors.

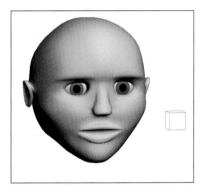

2. Select the right eye.

3. Choose *Animation > Constraints > LookAt Constraint,* and click the dummy object in front of the head.

   The eye rolls up into the head. In order for the look-at constraint to work, you must set the appropriate axis for the eye. The eyes were created in the Front viewport, so their local Z axes point straight ahead.

4. In the **Motion** panel, in the middle of the LookAt Constraint rollout, change the **Select Look-At Axis** to Z.

5. For the **aligned to Upnode Axis** option at the bottom of the rollout, choose Z.

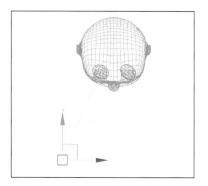

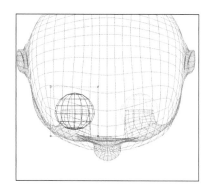

This will cause the eye to have the same orientation on its X and Y axes as it had before you added the look-at constraint.

6. Turn off **Viewline Length Absolute**.

   This makes the blue line extend all the way to the look-at target.

7. Select the left eye, and follow the same steps to set up a look-at constraint for the left eye.

8. In the Top viewport, move the dummy object to the left or right.

   When you move the dummy object way over to the left or right, you can see the eyes rotate in the Top viewport. There is a slight problem, though: If you watch the User viewport, you can see the edges of the eyes rotating into or out of the eye sockets at the extremes.

Create FFD Space Warps

To prevent the problem of the eyes popping out of their sockets as they rotate, you'll shape the eyes with an FFD space warp.

1. Load the file *CharAnimEyesFFD01.max*.

   This file contains the same setup, but the eyes haven't been shaped to fit the head.

2. On the **Create** panel, click ≋ **Space Warps**. Choose *Geometric/Deformable* from the drop-down menu, and click **FFD (Box)**.

3. Click **Set Number of Points**, and set **Length**, **Width**, and **Height** to 2.

4. In the Top viewport, click and drag to create a space warp around the right eye. Drag again to set the space warp's height, and click to finish creating it.

The space warp is shaped like a box, with a control point at each corner of the box. You'll use this box to warp the eye in a later step.

5. Use 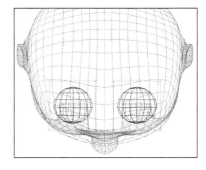 **Align** to align the space warp with the right eye.

6. On the **Modify** panel, name the space warp **SWEyeR**.

7. Set the space warp's **Length**, **Width**, and **Height** to 24.

   This will make the space warp sufficiently large to encompass the eye.

8. In the Deform group, choose the **All Vertices** option.

   This will cause the space warp to deform all vertices in the eye, even if they aren't inside the space warp. Setting this option makes the space warp work even if it's a little too small for the eye.

9. Make a copy of the space warp, and name it **SWEyeL**. Align this space warp with the left eye.

Bind the Eyes to the Space Warps

In order for a space warp to affect an object, you must bind the object to it.

1. Select the right eye. Make sure the eye itself is selected, not the space warp.

2. On the main toolbar, click **Bind to Space Warp**.

3. Press the [H] key, and choose **SWEyeR** from the Select Space Warp dialog.

   A new modifier, **FFD Binding**, appears on the stack for the right eye.

4. Select the left eye, and click **Bind to Space Warp**. Press the [H] key and choose **SWEyeL**.

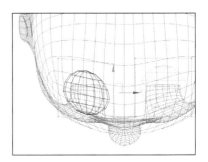

Warp the Eyes with the Space Warps

1. Select the space warp on the right eye.

2. On the 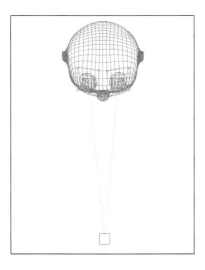 Modify panel, expand the listing to show the **Control Points** sub-object, and highlight it.

3. In the Top viewport, move the control points to skew the eye and make it follow the shape of the head, as shown in the picture.

   As you move the control points, you'll see the eye deforming to follow the shape of the lattice. Check your work in the User viewport to make sure the eye looks good.

4. Turn off **Control Points** when you have finished.

5. Select the space warp on the left eye. Use the control points on this space warp to skew the left eye in the direction opposite the right. Turn off **Control Points** when you have finished.

Set up the Look-At Constraint

Now you're ready to apply the look-at constraint to the eyes.

1. Select the right eye.

2. Choose *Animation > Constraints > LookAt Constraint*, and click the dummy object in front of the head.

3. In the **Motion** panel, set the **Select Look-At Axis** and the **aligned to Upnode Axis** to Z. Turn off **Viewline Length Absolute**.

4. Select the left eye, and follow the same steps to set up a look-at constraint on the left eye.

5. Move the dummy object to the left or right.

   The eyes follow the look-at target, but they stay deformed to the shape of the head as they turn.

6. Save the scene as **CharAnimEyesFFD02.max**.

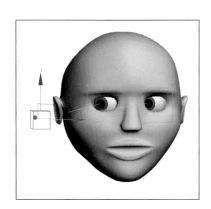

Facial Expressions and Speech

As with body animation, your best tool for facial animation is your own face. That said, your second-best tool is a mirror. Before you animate your character, make the faces yourself, and note how your facial muscles and features respond to each emotion. If you want to animate your character speaking, talk to your mirror and notice how your mouth moves to form each sound.

In this book, you'll learn to create facial expressions and animate them with the Morpher modifier. You'll also find out how these techniques can easily be used for speech animation.

Morpher Modifier

A good way to animate facial expressions and speech is to use a Morpher modifier to gradually change one version of an object into a different version.

To use the Morpher modifier with a character's head, you must first create several copies of the head, and arrange the vertices on each copy into different expressions. The various copies are called *morph targets*. Then you can apply the Morpher modifier to the head, and use it to animate the head changing to match specific morph targets on different frames.

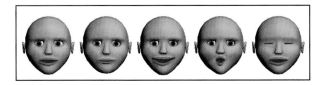

The Morpher modifier requires that all objects have the same number of vertices. So before you make any copies, you must take the time to set up the head with all the vertices you think you'll need. For example, if the character will open its mouth, the initial head must have a mouth cavity and sufficient vertices at the lips to form the expressions. If the character is going to blink, you must give it polygons that can act as eyelids.

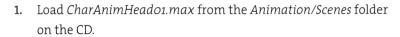

TUTORIAL A7

Morphing Facial Expressions

In this tutorial, you'll create several versions of a single head, model different facial expressions, and morph between them with the Morpher modifier. You can use this technique with any model to animate the character's face.

Load the Head Scene

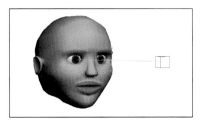

1. Load *CharAnimHead01.max* from the *Animation/Scenes* folder on the CD.

   This scene contains a single head with its mouth and eyes in a neutral pose. The eyes are rigged with FFD space warps to follow the dummy object when it moves.

2. Select **Head_Base**, the head in the scene.

   The head has **TurboSmooth** applied to it, because you'll need to see the results of **TurboSmooth** at certain times while you work. But you'll need to work at the **Editable Poly** level of the object.

3. On the **Modify** panel, turn off the 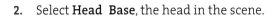 **Show end result on/off toggle** if it's still turned on.

Create a Mouth Cavity

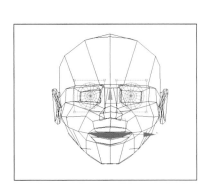

The head needs a mouth cavity so the facial expressions will look more realistic when the character opens its mouth. We'll assign a material to the polygons before we extrude them, so the mouth will have its own color that's applied as it's created. (See Chapter 1 if you need a refresher on creating materials or extruding polygons.)

1. In the Material Editor, select the **Head** material and set the number of materials to 3.

2. Change the last material to a dark red color, rename it to **Mouth Cavity**, and close the Material Editor.

3. Go to the **Polygon** sub-object level for the **Editable Poly**, and for the two polygons that make up the inside of the mouth, set **Material ID** to 3.

    When you extrude the selected polygons into the head, the new polygons will also have this material ID and material.

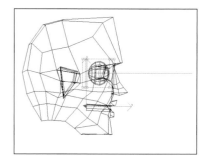

4. While watching the Left viewport, extrude the selected polygons into the character's head.

5. In the Edit Geometry rollout, click **Make Planar**.

    This straightens out the selected polygons, making them all lie in the same plane. This will make it easier to adjust the vertices in the steps that follow.

6. Turn on the **Show end result on/off toggle**.

7. Go to the **Vertex** sub-object level for the Editable Poly, select the vertices at the end of the mouth cavity, and scale them to make the inside of the cavity larger.

    Be sure to check your work in both the Front and Left viewports.

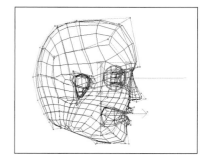

8. When you've finished, turn off the **Show end result on/off toggle** and turn off the **Vertex** sub-object level.

Create Copies of the Head

The Morpher modifier works only with objects that have the same number of vertices. The easiest way to create these objects is to make several copies of the base object, and move vertices on each one.

1. In the Front viewport, create four copies of the head to the right of the original.

    The head copies won't have any eyes. You'll use the **Morpher** modifier without affecting the eyes, so you don't need a set of eyes for each head.

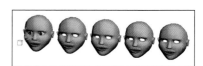

2. Name the copies **Head_CloseMouth**, **Head_Smile**, **Head_Ooo**, and **Head_Blink**.

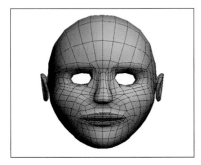

3. In the Top viewport, move each copy forward individually so you can see each one's profile in the Left viewport.

4. Save the scene as **CharAnimHead02.max**.

Create the First Facial Expression

1. In the Front viewport, zoom in on **Head_CloseMouth**.

2. Go to the ⬚ **Vertex** sub-object level for the **Editable Poly**, and turn on **Ignore Backfacing** in the Selection rollout.

3. Move vertices around the mouth area to close the mouth in a neutral expression.

4. Check your work in both the Left and Front viewports, and turn on the ⬚ **Show end result on/off toggle** as necessary to see how the facial expression looks with smoothing.

5. Turn off the ⬚ **Vertex** sub-object level when you're done so you can select the next head.

Create the Remaining Facial Expressions

For each facial expression, zoom in on the head in the Front viewport, turn on Ignore Backfacing, and work at the Vertex sub-object level. You might also find it useful to work in *Smooth + Highlights* mode with *Edged Faces* turned on. You can also use soft selection when working with sets of vertices to move entire regions of the face.

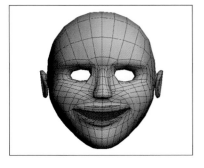

1. For **Head_Smile**, pose the mouth vertices into a smile. When you smile, the corners of your mouth not only move away from the center of your face, but they move slightly toward the back of your head. In addition, your lips flatten out to some degree.

    To make the smiling expression, move not just the vertices at the mouth, but also those on the nose, cheekbones, and eyes just a little bit. You can also move and rotate the vertices at the corners of the eyes to make the smile "reach" the eyes. This will make this expression look more natural during animation.

2. For **Head_Ooo**, pose the lips in a pucker, as if the character were saying, "Ooo." Push the bottom of the nose upward a little, and squint the eyes slightly.

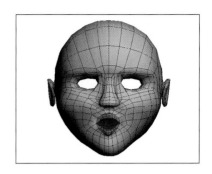

3. For **Head_Blink**, move the eyelids close together to close the eyes.

   This can be the trickiest expression to create. There are sets of vertices near the edges of the eyes specifically for closing the eyelids. You'll have to carefully select these vertices and move them up or down to close the eyes. Use *Wireframe* display, 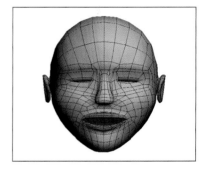 **Arc Rotate**, or any means necessary to find and select these vertices.

   You only have to adjust the eyelid vertices for this expression. When you use this expression with the **Morpher** modifier, you will use only the selection of vertices used to close the eyes, so you can combine this expression with others.

   Be sure to check your work with **TurboSmooth**, as the eyelids won't close as much when **TurboSmooth** is turned on.

4. On **Head_Blink**, select the vertices you moved to close the eyelids, and in the **Named Selection Sets** entry area, enter the name **Eyelids**.

   This creates a selection set that you will be able to access only when you are at the **Vertex** sub-object level. By creating this selection set, you ensure you'll be able to select the vertices again if you lose the selection by accident.

5. Turn off the ⊡ **Vertex** sub-object level for **Head_Blink**.

6. Save the scene as **CharAnimHead03.max**.

Apply the Morpher Modifier

You'll apply the Morpher modifier to Head_Base below its Turbo-Smooth modifier. The system will respond faster if it's morphing unsmoothed meshes, because they have fewer vertices.

1. Hide the space warps and dummy object to make it easier to see **Head_Base**.

2. Remove the **TurboSmooth** modifier from all the heads except **Head_Base**.

   When you ask the Morpher modifier to load morph targets, it will only find those that have the same number of vertices as Head_Base before TurboSmooth is applied. Therefore, you have to remove TurboSmooth from all the other heads before you can use them as morph targets.

3. Select **Head_Base**.

4. Select the **Editable Poly** level for **Head_Base**, and apply the **Morpher** modifier.

   Make sure the **Morpher** modifier appears below **Turbo-Smooth** on the stack.

5. In the Channels List rollout, click **Load Multiple Targets**. Select all the heads that appear on the list.

6. Save the scene as **CharAnimHead04.max**.

Morph the Facial Expressions

The Morpher modifier works with *channels*. In the Channel List rollout, each morph target appears in its own channel, only one per channel. You morph to different targets by animating the channel percentage. When a morph target's percentage is set to 100, the face takes on 100 percent of that facial expression.

1. Turn on **Auto Key**.

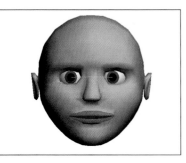

2. Go to frame 20, and set the percentage for **Head_CloseMouth** to 100.

   This morphs the head to match this morph target.

3. Go to frame 25, and set the percentage for **Head_CloseMouth** to 0.

4. On frame 25, set the percentage for **Head_Smile** to 100.

Keys for each percentage are stored separately, so the **Head_Smile** percentage will go from 0 to 100 over frames 0 to 25. To keep the character from smiling until frame 20, you'll have to set a key for this channel at frame 20.

5. Go back to frame 20, and change the percentage for **Head_Smile** to 0.

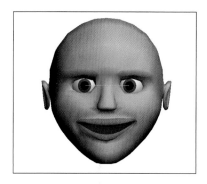

    Now you'll animate the eyes blinking around frame 25. You can tell the Morpher modifier to use only the last vertices selected to form the morph target for this channel.

6. Click **Head_Blink** in the Channel List rollout to select that channel. In the Channel Parameters rollout, turn on **Use Vertex Selection**.

7. Go to frame 25, and set the **Head_Blink** percentage to 100.

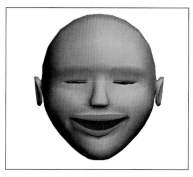

    The eyes close, but the smile expression doesn't change, because the channel is morphing only the selected vertices on the eyelids.

8. On frames 22 and 27, and set the **Head_Blink** percentage to 0.

    This creates a blink with three frames to close the eyes, and two frames to open them. If you play the animation, you'll see the character close its mouth, then smile and blink.

9. Save the scene as **CharAnimHead05.max**.

Finish the Animation

►TIP◄

If your system is running too slowly, make sure the TurboSmooth modifier is turned off.

Now you'll set up the remaining keys in preparation for using this head animation with a body animation sequence you created earlier.

1. Use ▣ **Time Configuration** to set the total number of frames to 120.

2. On frame 55, set **Head_CloseMouth** to 100 and **Head_Smile** to 0.

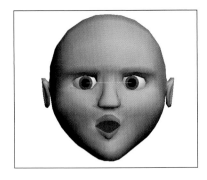

3. Go back to frame 50, and set **Head_CloseMouth** to 0 to keep the mouth closed until that frame. Set **Head_Smile** to 100.

4. Set the remaining keys in the following order:

Frame	Expression	Percentage
50	Head_Blink	100
47	Head_Blink	0
52	Head_Blink	0
85	Head_CloseMouth	0
85	Head_Ooo	100
80	Head_CloseMouth	100
80	Head_Ooo	0
80	Head_Blink	100
77	Head_Blink	0
82	Head_Blink	0
102	Head_CloseMouth	100
102	Head_Ooo	0
102	Head_Blink	100
100	Head_CloseMouth	0
100	Head_Ooo	100
100	Head_Blink	0

The animation should end with the character's eyes and mouth closed. If you like, you can play the animation to see what it looks like. If you don't want to set all these keys, you can load *CharAnimHead06.max* from the *Animation/Scenes* folder on the CD to see the final sequence.

5. If you removed the **TurboSmooth** modifier from **Head_Base**, turn it back on now.

6. Save the scene as **CharAnimHead06.max**.

►TIP◄

Any time the facial expression changes is a good time for a blink.

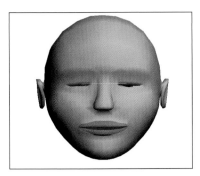

Animating Speech

You can use the same morphing techniques to make your character talk. Simply create a series of morph targets that represent 8–12 vowel and consonant sounds, and morph between them. Synchronize the morphs with a recorded soundtrack to make the character appear to talk.

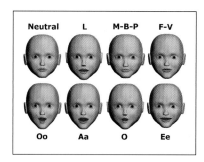

These sounds, and the facial positions that represent them, are called *phonemes.* You don't need a phoneme for every letter of the alphabet, because the mouth position is the same for many sounds. For example, your mouth looks nearly the same when you pronounce the letter *B* as it does for *P.*

If you wish to pursue this type of animation, consult a reference that covers this topic in detail. Some of these references are listed in the "Resources" section at the back of this book.

►TIP◄

You can find a list of phonemes and their corresponding facial positions in any comprehensive book on character animation. The phonemes are the same for both traditional and computer animation.

TUTORIAL A8

Merging Head and Body

Now you can merge the heads into a scene with an existing character rig, and use the facial expressions in conjunction with body animation.

Prepare the Head for Merging

To prepare the head for use in a scene, you'll link all the objects to a single object. Then you only have to link that one object to the character rig's head bone.

1. Load the file *CharAnimHead06.max* from the CD or continue from the previous exercise.

2. Hide all the heads except **Head_Base**.

3. Unhide the space warps and dummy object.

4. Create a dummy object about half the size of the head. Name the dummy object **DummyHeadAll**.

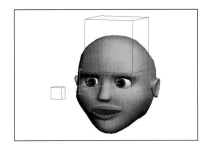

5. Move the dummy object so it sits just on top of the head.

6. Select all the objects in the scene except **DummyHeadAll** (the head, eyes, space warps, and look-at dummy), and link them to **DummyHeadAll**.

7. Test the linkage by moving **DummyHeadAll**. The head, eyes, space warps, and look-at dummy should move along with it.

8. Save the scene as **CharAnimHead07.max**.

Merge the Head into the Action Scene

1. Load the scene *CharAnimCatch03.max*, either your own version or the one from the *Animation/Scenes* folder on the CD.

2. Play the animation.

   This is a version of the scene you animated earlier, with the character waving his arms, getting hit by a ball, and falling down.

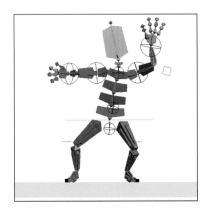

3. Unhide **Skater_Mesh_Head**, and delete it.

   This is the existing head in the scene. You'll be replacing this head with your morphed head, so you can get rid of it.

4. Choose *File > Merge,* and choose *CharAnimHead07.max*. Select all the objects in the scene, including the morph targets.

   Because you hid the morph targets before saving the scene, they come into the current scene already hidden.

Place the Head

1. Unhide the body and hair mesh objects.

2. On frame 0, move **DummyHeadAll** so the head sits on the head bone, **BoneHead**. If necessary, rotate it to match the rotation of **BoneHead**.

3. Unfreeze all the objects in the scene.

4. Link **DummyHeadAll** to **BoneHead**.

5. Link the hair mesh to **BoneHead**.

6. Hide all the bones and control objects.

7. If the neck protrudes into the mouth cavity, go to the 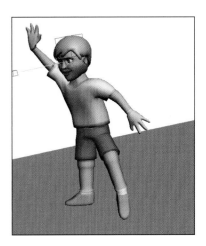 **Vertex** sub-object level of the body mesh's **Editable Poly**, and move the topmost neck vertices down to make the neck nub shorter.

   You can also improve the scene by changing the character's facial or body skin colors so they match.

▶TIP◀

To make colors match, you can drag a face or body color to the Color Clipboard utility to hold it. Then you can select the other material and drag the color from the Color Clipboard to the material.

8. Play or render the animation.

   The character smiles, blinks, and says "Ooo!" when he's about to catch the ball. When the ball hits him, he closes his eyes, and they remain closed for the duration of the animation.

   To get the facial timing for this animation, I looked for times when the character made a strong move, and changed his facial expression at those times. The blinks also coincide with strong motions.

9. Save the scene as **CharAnimCatch04.max**.

   You can find a version of this scene that includes lights and materials in the file *CharAnimCatch05.max* in the *Animation/Scenes* folder on the CD. There's also a rendered version called *CharAnimCatch05.avi* in the *Animation/AVI* folder.

   If you like, you can also animate the look-at dummy to make the character look in different directions over the course of the action.

Congratulations!

Now that you've gone through this book, you have all the tools you need to model, rig, and animate with 3ds max 7. Try out the techniques on your own characters, and use what you've learned to bring them to life.

I also encourage you to explore some of the resources listed at the back of this book to further your education in character animation. Good luck!

RESOURCES

Congratulations on making your way through this book. You now
know the basics of modeling, rigging, and animating characters
with 3ds max. I hope you're inspired to experiment and learn more!

There are many resources you can use to further your abilities,
whether you prefer books, DVDs, or surfing the Internet.

Books

Computer Animation

Mastering the Art of Production with 3ds max 4, Michele Bousquet
and Jason Busby

Modeling a Character with 3ds max, Paul Steed

Digital Character Animation, George Maestri

Character Animation, Doug Kelly

Traditional Character Design and Animation Principles

The Animator's Workbook, Tony White

How to Draw Cartoon Characters, Preston Blair

Timing in Animation, Harold Whitaker and John Halas

Acting for Animators, Ed Hooks

Animation from Script to Screen, Shamus Culhane

Disney Animation: The IIllusion of Life, Frank Thomas and Ollie Johnston

The Human Figure in Motion and *Animals in Motion,* Eadweard Muybridge

DVDs

These DVDs are available from Discreet. They provide a visual approach to learning about character modeling and animation with 3ds max.

Discreet Advanced Character Modeling

Discreet Character Rigging

Discreet Advanced Character Animation

Web Sites

For additional assistance, visit these resources on the Internet.

Discreet Support Forum	http://support.discreet.com
Maxhelp	www.maxhelp.com
CG Character	www.cg-char.com
3D Buzz	www.3dbuzz.com
CG Training	www.cgtraining.com
3D Luvr	www.3dluvr.com
3D Cafe	www.3dcafe.com

INDEX

S